D1443715

Revised Edition

the art of flute playing

by Edwin Putnik

Professor of flute, Arizona State University. Recitalist, clinician, and member of the Gammage Woodwind Quintet. Formerly with the Denver, Chicago, and Phoenix Symphonies, Chicago Lyric Theater Opera Orchestra, and former instructor of flute at the University of Illinois.

Summy-Birchard Inc.
exclusively distributed by
Warner Bros. Publications Inc.
15800 N.W. 48th Avenue
Miami, FL 33014

Copyright © 1970 Summy-Birchard Music
Division of Summy-Birchard, Inc.
exclusively distributed by
Warner Bros. Publications Inc.
Miami, Florida, U.S.A.
All rights reserved   Printed in U.S.A.

ISBN 0-87487-077-1
9 11 13 15 16 14 12 10

INTRODUCTION

Part I of this book is specifically designed to serve as a guide for the instruction of beginning students of the flute. With only a few exceptions, however, the concise principles presented here are valid for all levels of flute performance. Considerable emphasis is placed upon pedagogy at the beginning level, in the hope of helping the many non-flutists teaching in school music programs. Continuing development of such basic principles as tone and articulation, and the many aspects of artistic performance are treated in detail in Part II.

The instrument primarily considered throughout the first part of this work is the one most widely in use: the metal C flute with closed G♯ key, and either closed or open holes. Other types of flutes, including the piccolo, are considered in later chapters.

CONTENTS

Introduction

PART 1 BASIC PRINCIPLES AND PEDAGOGY

PART 2   ARTIST PERFORMANCE

BASIC PRINCIPLES AND PEDAGOGY

PART ONE

CHAPTER I

THE INSTRUMENT

THE FLUTE FAMILY

The oldest of the wind instruments, flutes, because of their essential simplicity have been known to all civilizations. They are basically of two types, distinguished by the manner of tone production:

1. The recorder group (fipple-flute, flûte à bec, etc.). In these the tone is produced by blowing into a mouthpiece, or fipple, which splits the air column, producing the tone.

2. The transverse flute, or cross flute, in which the tone is produced by blowing across a hole near one end of the flute. This latter type is the one considered here. The recorder family, although presently enjoying a revival of interest, does not have the popularity, practicality, or problems associated with it that the transverse flute has.

In the western world today, the flute family has narrowed down to five basic instruments.

CONCERT FLUTE (grand flute; F. *flûte*; G. *Grosse Flöte*; It. *flauto*). A non-transposing flute in the key of C, with a range from C^1 to D^4+. It is usually made of metal, with a cylindrical bore, or, still popular in some areas of Europe, made of wood with a conical bore.

PICCOLO (F, *petite flûte*; G. *Kleine Flöte*; It. *piccolo*, or *ottavino*). These are made of wood or metal, in C or Db, transposing up an octave or a minor ninth, respectively. The written range is from D^1 to C^4, and both conical and cylindrical bores are available.

Eb FLUTE (G. *Terz Flöte*). Somewhat smaller than the concert flute, it is becoming more and more popular in school band organizations. It is in the key of Eb, sounding a minor third higher than written, with a written range from C^1 to C^4+.

ALTO FLUTE (F. *flûte alto;* G. *Altflöte;* It. *flautone*). In the key of G, it sounds a fourth lower than written, with the same written range as the concert flute. Although the extreme high range is not very practical, the low and middle registers have a very full and mellow tone.

BASS FLUTE. In the key of C, it sounds an octave lower than written. It is difficult to play, because of the quantity of air required and the problems of adjusting to the embouchure hole. The written range is, again, the same as the concert flute, with the extreme high register somewhat impractical.

THE RANGE OF FLUTES

written   *sounding*

Concert Flute

same

Piccolo in C

Piccolo in Db

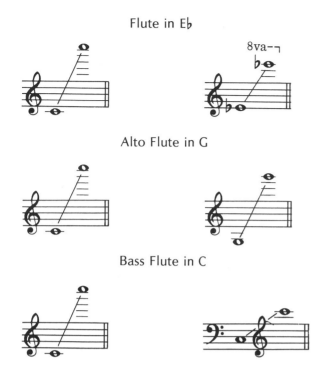

Flute in E♭

Alto Flute in G

Bass Flute in C

The concert flute is treated here. Details of the other instruments and their individual characteristics will be found in Chapter XI.

SELECTING AN INSTRUMENT

Thanks to the extensive work of Theobald Boehm in developing the modern flute, the purchaser may rely upon the product of any reputable manufacturer in selecting a student instrument. The mathematical proportions of the flute have been so carefully determined that the basic intonation and design are surprisingly reliable. Variants are mainly found in the approximate parabola of the bore of the head joint, and in the shape and size of the embouchure hole and plate.

The embouchure plate varies principally in its curvature or arc, and the resultant distance from the body of the head joint. In earlier models, there apparently was an attempt to approximate the outer diameter of wood flutes, so that the change from one to the other would be easier. In more recent years, the tendency has been toward a slightly smaller arc, which has proved more universally desirable. In selecting an instrument for the beginning student, however, this need not be of concern. The variation is minimal and the student must develop his embouchure before he is capable of trying the various styles and selecting the model most satisfactory for himself.

Embouchure holes have developed along two basic designs: one based on an oval and one based on a rounded rectangle. The basic oval design is closer to the shape of the embouchure holes found on most early wood flutes, and was quite common when metal flutes were first developed. The rounded rectangle, however, has proved to be more satisfactory in developing contemporary tonal concepts. The arc of the far edge of

the embouchure hole, upon which the air column is split, is more in accordance with the ideal shape of the air column when the hole is based on the shape of a rectangle, due to the horizontal elongation of the flute embouchure.

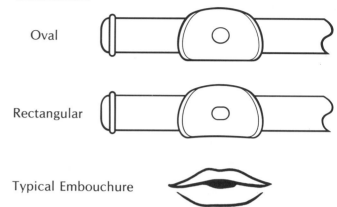

Oval

Rectangular

Typical Embouchure

A comparison of embouchure holes on several student flutes will immediately give the purchaser a concept of the average size of the embouchure hole. Any significant variation from this average is not recommended for the beginner, although many experiments in this regard have been promoted by both manufacturers and flutists. The advantages of a larger or smaller embouchure hole, unfortunately, have their offsetting disadvantages, making them undesirable for the beginning student. A larger hole makes the lower register easier to produce, a tempting characteristic for the novice, but it also makes the high register extremely difficult to control, or even to sound. The smaller hole allows for easier control and production of sound in the middle and high octaves. But the low register is thin in tone, and may even prove impossible for the beginner.

Materials used in flutes have included all substances capable of holding a shape: wood, metal, glass, plastic, jade, ceramic, stone, bone, etc. The manufacture of flutes today, however, is confined to wood, such as ebony or grenadilla, and several metals. Wood flutes are still used in a few European orchestras, but metal instruments have supplanted them in most of the western world, due to their superior brillance and projection of tone. [1]

Several choices in combinations of metals are available in student flutes, usually in the material of the tube and head joint, and the kind of plating. The beginner's flute is usually a brass tube with a choice of nickel or silver plate. The effect on tone production is negligible, and the choice between them is based on other minor factors. Nickel plate is harder, more durable, shinier, and takes almost no care. When the nickel plate wears off, however, it is usually not practical to have it redone. Silver plate has a softer luster, but it does tarnish, and requires more care. When it eventually wears off, however, it can be reapplied.

---

[1]The sweet, mellow quality of the wood flute, however, might well be reinvestigated for its possibilities in some solo and ensemble literature.

At the next price level in student flutes, there is a wide choice in combinations of materials. The entire flute tube, or the head joint alone, may be obtained in sterling silver, or in a silver alloy. The key mechanism may be obtained in nickel silver, with or without silver plate, or entirely in silver. Each step toward a completely silver flute adds to the quality of the instrument. The silver head joint improves tone quality and response, the entire tube in silver is still better. And the addition of silver keys avoids the problems of plating, although nickel silver keys are entirely satisfactory. The finest flutes usually employ a silver alloy, sometimes called coin silver, rather than sterling. The alloy's hardness encourages brilliance and response, and may be drawn finer in construction.

Artist flutes are most often made of a silver alloy throughout, including keys and mechanism, with the added feature of gold springs. To avoid the extreme tendency to tarnish, due to the body chemistry of some players, a gold-plated embouchure plate is often desirable.

Some of the finest flutes made in recent years have been entirely of a gold alloy, or of platinum. The greater density of these metals improves the flute's tone quality and response, but their cost is beyond the budget of the average flutist.

There are several other features of flute design that should be familiar to the purchaser, though most of them do not affect the total price of the instrument. Flutes are still available with either a closed or open G♯ key, although the closed G♯ model is almost exclusively in use today. The open G♯ key was the original design of Boehm, and did have some advantages in tone and control. But the reverse action of the closed key allows for simpler fingering in the high register.

The G key is also available on many flutes in either an offset or in a straight-line design. The offset G key is recommended for most beginners, since it enables the young student to reach this key more easily with the ring finger of the left hand. The straight-line design, however, is preferred by almost all professional flutists because of the simpler method of manufacture.

Straight Line

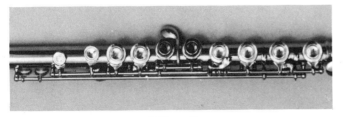

Offset G

Ribbed construction of post mountings is recommended, rather than the method in which the posts that support the flute mechanism are directly fastened to the body of the flute. This latter method requires a thicker flute tube, which is not desirable. It also lacks the strength and security of the ribbed method, in which the posts are fastened to bars or ribs of metal attached to the flute tube.

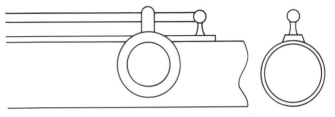

Ribbed Mounting

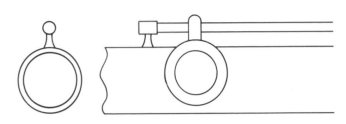

Direct Mounting

Also affecting the thickness of the flute tube is the way the tone holes are made. Most student flutes have drawn tone holes, in which the pad seats are drawn up out of the tube in a one-piece construction. This is desirable because of the strength it affords and because it avoids possible leaks due to faulty seams.

Most professional flutes, however, have pad seats that are attached to the flute tube individually, allowing for a thinner tube. The process of drawing tone holes takes metal from the tube itself, so the tube must be thicker to afford this type of construction. Although the thinner tube is desired by most artists, because of the ease of response and additional brilliance, drawn tone holes encourage a more economical construction, so they are found in most student flutes.

If the student purchases a flute with drawn tone holes, he should also see that the edges of the tone holes are rolled—that is, turned over to provide a wider seat for the pads. Tone holes that are not rolled will cut the pads in very short order, requiring frequent replacement of pads.

Drawn and Rolled Tone Hole

Plastic pads have been a recent development in flute manufacture and offer good and bad features to be considered in selecting a flute. While they are easier to seat originally and normally last longer than bladder pads, they tend to respond in a spongy fashion. And the student soon indents them on the pad seat so that they tend to grab the rim of the tone hole and retard key action.

Although repairmen and manufacturers seem to favor plastic pads, because of the ease and economy in installing them, bladder pads are still desirable for the flutist.

Most flute manufacturers also offer a choice of open or closed holes even in their student model flutes. The open hole, or French model, flute is desirable because of its even scale, good intonation, and ease of control in the upper register. For these reasons, it is the type of flute used by almost all professionals.

Closed holes, however, are easier for the beginner to manage, and absolutely necessary for the youngster whose hands have not yet fully grown. The problem of covering these holes can be solved by using plugs that are available through most manufacturers. These may be removed later, one at a time, as the student becomes accustomed to the instrument.

The French model flute is therefore recommended for any serious student, to avoid an often difficult change at a later date.

Student flutes should also have four or five adjustment screws to control the action where one key operates additional keys. These are usually found between the B♭ and A keys in the left hand, and controlling the action of the F♯ key in relation to each of the keys in the right hand. There may also be an adjustment screw on the B♭ connection to the F key, and this is desirable on student flutes.

Some manufacturers, unfortunately, have included several additional adjusting screws, so that the player can adjust them more easily. The fact is, though, that the flute tends to be almost continually out of adjustment. Artist flutes, primarily handmade, will normally have no adjusting screws because of problems in manufacture. This makes the flute harder to adjust initially, but it will maintain the adjustment much longer.

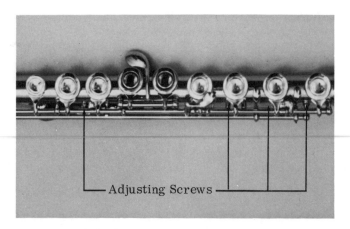

—— Adjusting Screws ——

Several optional keys and other features, available on most flute models, will be considered here, although

their specific uses will be treated in detail in later chapters.

B♭ lever: Enables the forefinger of the right hand to operate the B♭ key. Although only useful in some trill and turn combinations, and in chromatic scales, this key is standard on most flutes.

B♮ lever: Offered only as an alternate to the above, it enables the forefinger of the right hand to operate the B♮ (thumb) key. This slight advantage is not as desirable as the B♭ lever, and is seldom used today.

Split E key: Used to counteract the closed G♯ key to improve production of E^3, but adding an unnecessary complication to the mechanism, since this tone should be no problem to the accomplished flutist.

Low B foot joint: A longer foot joint, making it possible to produce the note B, one semitone below the normal range of the flute. The B key is activated by the little finger of the right hand on an extra roller. The value of this extra note is somewhat questionable, but the addition to the length of the flute does increase resistance and security in the high register, and is often recommended.

High C gizmo (C^4): A small tab on the low B key, allowing it to be closed without closing the other keys on the foot joint. Its only value is easier production and better intonation of the highest C.

C♯ trill: An extra hole and reverse-action key operated by the forefinger of the right hand. The facility gained in trills to C♯ is of small value, but the key does afford a magnificent trill from G^3 to A^3, which otherwise is somewhat disappointing. This slight advantage, however, is offset by the confusion of adding another lever to the right hand, and by the tendency, since it is a reverse-action key, to encourage a leak in the flute.

Several other keys are available on flutes to facilitate the action of the ring finger or little finger on either hand, such as a G trill activated by the right hand, or a low C or B lever in the left hand. In every instance, these are not recommended unless there are physical problems that make these extra keys desirable or necessary.

MAINTENANCE

The most important point in flute care is to keep it clean and as free of moisture as possible. The inside of the flute should swabbed after use with a small, clean cloth that may be tucked into the cleaning rod provided with the flute.

The outside of the flute should also be wiped with a cloth before returning it to the case, where this moisture cannot rapidly evaporate. Care must be taken, however, to avoid (a) a circular motion on the keys, as this tends to loosen the mechanism, throwing the flute out of adjustment, and (b) any friction on the pads themselves. Removing this moisture will prevent most tarnish buildup and help increase the life of the pads. Resting the flute with the mechanism up will also help keep the moisture from the pads.

The use of metal polish of any type is definitely not recommended, unless applied by a skilled craftsman. A competent repairman will clean the instrument in a cyanide bath when it is completely overhauled, which should be the only time such measures are necessary. The use of polish is extremely hazardous—it may ruin the mechanism and pads alike. The buildup of tarnish may be retarded by keeping a tarnish-preventing cloth, which is commercially available, or a small piece of camphor in the flute case.

A word of caution is necessary in reference to buffing the head joint: The embouchure plate and hole may easily be ruined by machine buffing, and an incompetent cleaning attempt may easily destroy the value of an otherwise satisfactory flute.

The assembly joints of the flute deserve special care, since they receive considerable wear in assembling and disassembling the flute. Twisting the joints when moving them in or out will avoid the danger of not getting them perfectly aligned. Take care not to grasp the rods of the instrument in the process, and keep the joints absolutely clean to avoid the extra wear caused by dust and grime.

Under ordinary circumstances, it should not be necessary to use cork grease, cold cream, or paraffin on these joints. If they are too tight, or perhaps worn to the point where there is not a good seal, cork grease may be used until the joints are corrected by a repairman. This grease must be wiped off frequently and replaced to prevent the buildup of dust that will accelerate the wear.

Note here that the joint protector caps furnished with some flutes, are only intended to prevent the grease from rubbing off in the case. They protect the case, not the flute, and in most instances are not necessary.

Occasionally cold weather will cause the flute sections to be unusually tight. This can be overcome by expanding the outer joints by breathing into the top of the body joint and the foot joint before assembling the flute.

Depending on the amount of use, the flute should also be oiled about once a month. A high-grade key oil or watchmaker's oil should be applied carefully to all friction points in the mechanism. To avoid damage to the pads, immediately remove any excess oil with a cloth. The amount of oil to be applied at each point is considerably less than a drop, and it can be done with the tip of an instrument screwdriver or a toothpick.

Sticking pads are usually the result of moisture and/or dirt, if the pad is not excessively worn or split. In emergencies, this can be relieved by inserting a corner of a clean handkerchief or piece of lightweight paper under the pad and drawing it through several times while applying light pressure to the key. Sometimes it may be necessary to wet the cloth with the tongue first, and then dry the pad.

In extreme situations, dirty pads may be cleaned with a small amount of alcohol on a cloth, again followed by drying the pad with a clean cloth. The use of talcum powder to relieve sticking pads is not wise, because moisture soon causes a paste to form that makes the pad stickier than before.

Beyond these measures, basic flute care includes only some minor points of emergency repair that the flutist should be familiar with. The problems most frequently plaguing flutists, besides sticky pads mentioned above, are improperly seated pads, poor adjustment of the action, or slow, sticky mechanism.

Pads that are properly seated when installed will not lose their seating unless excessive moisture causes them to change shape. A pad that has thus warped must be replaced by a repairman. More common, however, is the problem of pads that do not cover because of a maladjustment in the action. This will be in the B♭ or F♯ key because of the dependence on the action of the other keys. Where adjusting screws are available at these points (see page 4), the remedy is immediately apparent. Otherwise a bit of paper glued to the worn cork will temporarily correct the problem. Careful observation in gently depressing the A, F, E, and D keys will show up the problem, as the attached keys must close at exactly the same instant.

Almost all instances of sluggish mechanical action on a flute, other than periodic wear, are the result of neglect. This may be due to corrosion, allowing moisture to remain in the instrument after use, or the result of allowing metal polish to get into the mechanism. Periodic oiling and daily wiping should prevent this problem, although sometimes an application of penetrating oil will be necessary before the action can be freed, if there has been some corrosion.

If these measures do not free the action, have a repairman disassemble the flute, clean the action, oil it, and readjust it. Under no circumstances should the springs be tightened to compensate for sluggish action; bending them to increase tension only shortens their life.

CHAPTER II

PLAYING POSITION

ASSEMBLY

The seemingly small point of the proper alignment of the three sections of the flute is so frequently mentioned only in passing in flute methods—or, worse, ignored completely—that we should give it all possible emphasis here. Innocent errors can seriously hamper a student's development of both sound and technique. And so the instructor will do well to check this point at the start of each instruction period until the basic alignment is another well-developed habit in the student's background.

Based on the average flutist's requirement (which is always the guide for the beginning student), the head joint is lined up with the middle joint in such a way that the embouchure hole is in a direct line with the first key (except trill keys) on the middle section.

To aid in this alignment, corresponding marks should be lightly scratched on these two sections of the instrument, after the correct alignment has been established by sighting down the flute. Some manufacturers include in their flute design such marks for alignment. These are helpful, but must be checked for accuracy before they can be used as a guide.

The essential purpose of this alignment is to ensure maximum freedom for finger dexterity by allowing the hands to hold the flute in the most natural position. Contrary to common belief, changes in this alignment, except in extreme instances, will not affect the beginning student's embouchure placement. Instead, the student will compensate for incorrect alignment by turning the flute in or out with his hands, resulting in awkward and unsteady hand positions.

As the alignment recommended is correct in the vast majority of instances, it is to be maintained for all students. A minor adjustment is only occasionally advisable, and even then not until the student is relatively advanced and his embouchure is considerably developed.

The foot joint is aligned so that the rod on this section is approximately in line with the center of the last key (D) on the middle joint. Here again, the purpose is to allow the most natural hand position and resulting maximum finger dexterity, based on the fact that the little finger is normally considerably shorter than its neighbor.

Improper alignment of the foot joint will seriously impair the development of finger technique in the right hand. It may also prevent proper development of the embouchure because of lack of support for the flute. If the foot joint is turned too far up, the student is forced to let the other fingers of the right hand extend beyond the keys in enabling the little finger to reach its lever. If the joint is turned too far down, the little finger cannot properly depress the keys, making facile technique an impossible goal.

HAND AND ARM POSITION

The prime consideration in holding the flute is to support it in the most natural and comfortable position compatible with finger freedom, steady support, and freedom to breathe properly.

These objectives are best attained by holding the flute approximately horizontal, with the upper arms free of the body, and the head held up and turned to the left about 30 degrees to allow a more comfortable position for the arms and shoulders. The reasons here are twofold: (1) proper breathing is impossible with the chest area constricted by the upper arms resting on the body; (2) allowing the arms to drop will cause the flute to shift in relationship to the student's lips, disturbing the embryo embouchure he is trying so hard to develop.

It is extremely important that the beginning flutist be constantly reminded to maintain this position. The temptation to rest the elbows against the body, or the arms on the back of a chair is so strong that the student must be sufficiently impressed with the correct position to maintain it in spite of some discomfort.

Realizing that it is somewhat tiring for the younger student to maintain this position for long periods of time, it is recommended that the beginner practice in several short periods of fifteen to twenty minutes daily rather than attempt longer practice sessions. In band or orchestra rehearsals this need not be a problem, for the student is seldom playing constantly for long periods of time. He will probably get more tired from sitting still than from holding up his flute.

Support for the flute is obtained mainly at three points: the base of the left forefinger, the thumb of the right hand, and the right little finger. The chin is, of course, an aid in support, but it must not be depended on for support, since pressure against the jaw will seriously disturb the embouchure.

The flute rests at the base of the left forefinger as illustrated, with this finger comfortably curved so that its tip can activate the key. Support in the right hand is achieved by the combination of the right thumb and the little finger. The thumb must support the flute from below. It is placed approximately under the first and second fingers, with the flute resting in the middle of the first joint of the thumb.

If the thumb protrudes excessively, the fingers above will be cramped; if it is too far back, support will be lacking. If the thumb is too far to the left or the right, the fingers will lean accordingly, and will be unable to move freely.

The left wrist should be somewhat bent and under the flute, while the right wrist is almost straight.

The individual student's hand is to be taken into account, but extreme variations in this basic position will impede finger action as well as interfere with the embouchure. Only minor adjustments of hand position, therefore, are to be tolerated.

Two common problems in this regard should be noted: First, some students are unable to bend their thumbs to oppose the fingers with the pad of the first joint. Instead, the side of the thumb is used to support the flute, but this need not present a problem if the student does not let the forefinger grasp the trill key rod. Second, many students today are encouraged to start playing the flute before they have grown enough to hold it properly. When the hands are too small, the student is forced to gain support for the instrument by wrapping the right forefinger around the mechanism.

For the small child, there is no solution, but this practice must be discouraged as soon as the child's hand is large enough to achieve the proper position. The concept of holding a ball or an orange in the right hand is helpful in conveying the idea of the proper position.

A word of caution at this point on the use of the *crutch*, as recommended by some manufacturers, to aid in supporting the flute. This device only succeeds in hampering the movement of the fingers in the left hand. If a student's flute includes one, the socket into which it screws should be removed, as well as the crutch itself. If permitted to remain, this socket will interfere with correct hand position, forcing the student to support the flute with considerable difficulty.

All of these considerations in hand position are of such importance that they deserve constant checking and correction. Errors here will show up as countless problems of technique and tone alike, often causing the instructor to look in the wrong area for solutions to students' faults and difficulties.

True, correct hand and arm position is at times troublesome for the beginner to achieve. But the amount of care and constant attention required of both student and teacher to ensure these necessary habits does not compare with the effort necessary to correct improper habits at a later date.

FINGER POSITION

The right little finger should reach the D♯ lever with ease and, together with the thumb, help support the flute. A moment's review of the basic fingering chart (p. 26) will remind the reader that this key is depressed on all tones from E♭^{1} through A^3, with the exception of middle D (D^2).

In only a few instances does this key affect tonal quality or intonation; it is held down primarily for steady support of the instrument. Because the little finger is not independent of the ring, or third, finger, the student will at first find it quite hard to keep the little finger depressed. But he should make every effort to do so. The student who is allowed to develop the habit of ignoring the right little finger will be denied even the smallest amount of technical facility in his right hand. And he will seriously postpone embouchure development through unsteady support of the flute.

The remaining fingers of the right hand should be curved, with their tips resting lightly on the keys. These fingers must not be allowed to rest against the action rods, or facility will be impaired. This usually occurs when the student is trying to support the flute more securely, and correction of the position of the right thumb and little finger is called for.

In the left hand, the fingers should also be curved, with their tips activating the keys. The left wrist must be turned in enough to allow the fingers to reach their keys comfortably. If the third and fourth fingers do not quite reach, the entire hand will be moved each time these fingers are called into action. This is an impossibly slow process that will also tend to jar the flute's position in relation to the lips.

For similar reasons, the left little finger should remain poised above its lever, rather than be allowed to drop below. Constant attention on the part of both instructor and student will be required to achieve these aims.

CHAPTER III

BASIC EMBOUCHURE

The acoustical facts and theories on producing sound on the flute are excellently considered in other writings, and need not be of concern here. Of immediate significance, however, is how flutists, as students, instructors, and performers, produce that sound, control it, and improve upon it.

Basically, a sound can be produced by blowing partly into and partly across the embouchure hole of the flute. A minimum of experiment here will produce a noise on the flute; refinement of that noise into a tone capable of musical expression is the next concern.

In blowing a small stream of air through the lips, the natural tendency is to pucker in the attempt to direct and control that air stream. This normally results in a round aperture in the lips and correspondingly shaped air stream. This, when applied to the flute, will produce a tone containing extraneous wind or hiss — too much air is inefficiently striking the edges of the embouchure hole.

To use the air column more effectively and avoid unpleasantly windy sounds, the corners of the mouth are drawn back slightly, elongating the shape of the aperture to:

Contrary to popular opinion, or perhaps rumor, this does not resemble the approach to playing tunes on a pop bottle, nor does it resemble a smile. For reasons to be made apparent later, the upper lip, in forming a flute embouchure, should be firm, and the lower lip somewhat looser or fleshier.

Generally, this is best accomplished by drawing the corners of the mouth straight back, or even down, rather than up as you would in a smile. In most cases, satisfactory tone production will be prevented by pulling the corners up, consequently stretching the lower lip.

In adjusting this basic mouth formation to the embouchure hole on the flute, there are two prime factors to be considered and developed: (1) where the air stream is centered and (2) how much of the embouchure hole the lower lip covers.

The stream of air must be centered in relation to the far edge of the embouchure hole. In most instances, the aperture in the lips will naturally form in the center of the mouth, or nearly so, and the embouchure hole may be centered accordingly by moving the flute to the right or left as needed. Since the air stream is usually directed straight out from the lips, this alignment should prove sufficient and easily accomplished.

Generally, the flute should also be held parallel to the line formed by the juncture of the lips. In cases where the student's lips rise higher at one corner or the other, or the head is tilted, the foot joint end of the flute should be raised or lowered correspondingly.

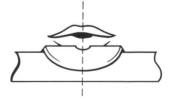

Note that the most comfortable position for holding the flute is usually at a slight angle below the horizontal, with the head slightly tilted accordingly. Note also that the position of the arms in playing the flute is somewhat unnatural, and often very tiring. This results, unfortunately, in a tendency to let the arms drop as the player tires. The elbows tend to come in toward the body rather than straight down, and this results in the player's tendency to push the flute continually to the left and distort the embouchure in the same direction. This can happen very gradually over a long period of time, so that the player is not conscious of the shift of embouchure.

Almost all instances of an uncentered aperture in the lips are found on the flutist's left side, and most often are the result of this tendency to push the flute over with the arms.

In any case, the solution is found in frequent checks before a mirror to center the embouchure and correct the angle of the flute in relation to the lips.

The column of air must be split approximately in half by the far edge of the embouchure hole. This adjustment often requires constant and considerable effort by both teacher and student before satisfactory tone and control are achieved.

In principle, the flute is placed so that an average of one-fourth to one-third of the embouchure hole is covered by the lower lip. If too little of the embouchure hole is covered, the resulting tone tends to be empty or shallow in quality. It will also necessitate an even greater quantity of air to produce sound, and will make tone production in the highest octave most difficult and solely dependent on overblowing.

Covering too much of the embouchure hole results in a tone that is small and thin in quality. It also limits the response to attack, legato facility, and range of dynamic variation. To produce a sound in this manner, however, requires a relatively small quantity of air and so it is a tempting pitfall for students and must be continually guarded against.

Having adjusted the lips to cover approximately the correct amount of the embouchure hole, it is then necessary to turn the flute in or out to discover the best angle for producing a tone. Because jaw formations vary considerably from one student to the next, a good deal of experiment and individual adjustment are often needed.

Fortunately, the instructor can see the relationship of lips to embouchure plate by looking carefully down the end of the flute as the student sustains tones. And the student can rely chiefly on the tactile sense of his lips in establishing and adjusting this relationship.

Also bear in mind that the amount of embouchure hole covered by the lip, and the angle at which the flute is held, are intricately and proportionately related to each other and to the average angle at which the air stream is directed from the flutist's lips.

Either moving the flute down on the lips or turning it in will cause the flutist to cover more of the hole, whereas raising the placement of the flute on the lip or turning it out will result in covering less hole. The effectiveness of these adjustments depends on the angle, as well as size and shape, of the air stream. Finding the best angle and placement for the flute will require considerable experiment.

To ensure placing the flute in exactly the same place on the lips every time, many students and professionals find it helpful to place the entire embouchure hole against both lips first, then turn the flute down to the proper angle.

This angle may best be found by sustaining tones in the range in which they are most easily produced, then turning the flute in and out gradually. The best angle for

the moment will be readily apparent to the ear, and may prove to be the only adjustment necessary.

If, however, the tonal quality suggests that less of the hole, for example, should be covered, the student will next move the flute up slightly on his lower lip. Generally, he will now have to turn the flute slightly (probably in), to reestablish the best angle for the flute in relation to the angle of the air stream.

Continued efforts of this nature will shortly demonstrate the most promising embouchure placement for each stage of the student's progress.

To produce a variety of sounds, infinite adjustments of this basic embouchure are necessary. In principle, the lower in range or in pitch, or the louder one plays, the more the air stream must be directed down into the instrument and the less the hole should be covered.

As one plays higher or softer, he must cover more of the embouchure hole and the air column should be directed more across that hole. This is apparently because a lower or louder tone requires a wider aperture in the lips and correspondingly larger air column, necessitating a downward adjustment to maintain the correct proportional split of the air column on the far edge of the embouchure hole. The converse is also true.

To accomplish the many requisite changes in the direction and size of the air column demands careful alterations in the relationship of the upper and lower lips to each other and to the embouchure hole on the flute.

Although students will often be tempted to make these adjustments in direction by rolling the flute in and out, or by bobbing the head up and down, neither solution proves practicable. Both methods constantly change the relative amount of embouchure hole covered by the lip in the opposite way to what is needed, thus altering or even stopping the tone.

In addition, these methods, even when accompanied by compensating changes in lip tension, are too slow for rapid interval changes and too inexact for practical use.

The only satisfactory method for embouchure adjustment in performance, relative to pitch, range, and intensity, is to exploit the control offered by the correct use of the lower jaw to alter the direction and shape of the air stream.

USE OF THE JAW

By bringing into play a fore and back movement of the lower jaw, the direction of the air column can be effectively governed. Stated simply, the lower in range or in pitch, or the louder one plays, the more he must draw the lower jaw back, not down. As the flutist goes up in range or in pitch, or diminishes in intensity, the jaw is thrust forward.

This movement of the jaw neatly serves several purposes: changes in the air stream's direction are accomplished with corresponding adjustments of the amount of embouchure hole covered, the size of the aperture, the openness of the throat, and the relative lip tension.

Thus, by bringing the jaw forward in diminuendo, for example, we reduce the size of the aperture, cover more hole, adjust the direction of the air stream to maintain quality, and keep the pitch level.

You can readily see that this use of the jaw truly makes possible more confident, facile, and exact changes of pitch, range, and intensity than can be achieved in any other fashion. In time, the performer can develop a certainty in this jaw action that is suggestive of the slide positions of the trombone, with, of course, infinitely more variation. Any specific note symbol, with accompanying dynamic indication or intent, stimulates a corresponding reflex adjustment of the jaw in preparation for the tone.

The beginning student, however, need only be concerned with the use of the jaw in controlling the several registers of the flute. He should begin this study with the slow practice of octaves, in which the lowest tone of those octaves with the same fingering is sounded first, then the jaw is brought forward until the upper octave sounds. These studies are best slurred, but the beginner may find it necessary to tongue them in his first trials.

INTONATION

Since the jaw is of prime importance in governing intonation on the flute, a few words on this subject for beginning students are in order. The instructor is urged to be both tolerant and cautious, because intonation to the beginner is a problem more of embouchure development and mental awareness than of adjusting the instrument itself.

The dimensions of the flute are standardized enough so that the product of any reputable manufacturer is reasonably well made in regard to intonation. In most cases, the flute is proportioned so that the pitch A^1, of 440 vibrations per second, may be sounded with the head joint pulled out of the middle joint about an eighth of an inch. This allows enough margin to adjust to the normal pitch variations found between instrumental groups or, in some cases, from day to day within the same group.

Beyond the small variation allowed by setting the head joint in or out (*in* raises the pitch, *out* lowers it), intonation depends principally upon the embouchure of the flutist. Basically, the pitch will be lowered by blowing more directly into the embouchure hole, or raised by blowing more across it.

Correct embouchure on the part of the flutist will produce tones closely in tune with the setting of the flute itself. The minor variations in pitch necessary during every performance are accomplished by the use of the jaw as discussed above, rather than by turning the flute in or out.

When considering intonation difficulties of beginning students (but no others) a tolerant attitude is advisable. Pitch, being so dependent upon embouchure, will vary considerably with students in the process of developing that embouchure. The instructor should concentrate on correcting problems of basic embouchure, and he will soon be pleased to discover that the tendency to play extremely flat or sharp has largely corrected itself.

The intonation problems of the student, moreover, can be a valuable guide to the instructor in locating and correcting embouchure faults. Generally, the student that continually plays flat is probably blowing down into the flute at too great an angle, while also covering too much of the embouchure hole.

Conversely, blowing too much across the embouchure hole, usually accompanied by covering too little of the hole, will cause the student to play quite sharp. In either case, the pitch will suggest the difficulty, and the necessary correction of lip formation and/or jaw position can be made.

Caution is advised when a student is tempted to compensate for extreme intonation problems by adjusting the flute rather than the embouchure. Minor adjustments of basic pitch should be made by setting the head joint as mentioned above. The head joint, however, is not simply a tuning slide, and if it is pulled out too far, will prevent the very production of sound on the flute.

Caution is again in order on tampering with the cork, or stopper, in the head joint. This cork alters the relative pitch of the registers, and is normally set seventeen millimeters from the center of the embouchure hole. To establish this setting, a mark is usually scored that distance from the end of the cleaning rod included in the flute case.

If this cork is set closer to the embouchure hole the pitch will be raised in the high register and simultaneously lowered slightly in the lowest octave. Setting it farther away from the embouchure hole will lower the pitch in the top octave and raise it somewhat in the lower.

These adjustments of the cork, however, should never be necessary for the novice. The student's role is to attempt to develop his embouchure in accordance with the average setting of the head cork. Only after the embouchure is reasonably well developed should any change from the normal setting of this cork, if still necessary, be attempted. If the cork is set too far from the norm it will seriously impair, if not prevent, the production of sound as well as its quality.

Finally, it should never prove necessary to have a piece of the head joint cut off to raise the pitch. Again, if the instrument is of reputable and recent origin, the fault lies with the flutist, not with the flute!

CHAPTER IV

BASIC ARTICULATION

SINGLE TONGUE

Starting a tone on the flute by merely blowing into it, although possible, is a technique rarely used in performance, and best never practiced by the beginning student. The tone is most often started by establishing the requisite air pressure in the mouth cavity, then releasing this air by means of the tongue. In essence, this is done by moving the tongue to form an inaudible *tah*, which is preferable to other syllables, in that it emphasizes the use of the tip of the tongue while also encouraging a more open throat in the attack.

You will notice in this basic attack that the tongue normally touches the gum just above and behind the upper front teet. This is the average position of the tongue in attack, and is the approach to be stressed with beginning students.

In further developing this basic attack, the following generalities may serve as guides. Note, though, that these generalities are intended primarily as a guide for beginning students; variants of the single attack, as well as other types of articulation, are discussed in Chapter VIII.

1. Only the tip of the tongue is to be used in this basic attack; any variation will not produce as clean or acute an attack.

2. The tongue should strike nearer to the edge of the upper incisors as one plays lower in range or louder in intensity, and strike higher up on the gum as one plays higher in range or softer.

In attacking the lowest tones, the tongue may even touch the lips, but take care that the tongue is not allowed to protrude between the lips. If it does protrude between attacks, it disturbs the embouchure so that the attack often has a distinct sound of its own, which is only then followed by the tone.

3. The tongue is used to start tones, not stop them. In articulating repeated tones, the preparation of the tongue for starting one tone will, of necessity, cut off the previous tone. The double-acting "tut-tut" sound of the tongue, frequently the result of misguided attempts at staccato, is very limited in its application to music, and is definitely not recommended for beginning students.

The student should concentrate on starting the tone with a clean attack, and stopping it, when not immediately followed by another tone, by simply interrupting the air stream.

4. The student should strive for evenness of attack in relation to the tone that follows. Tones beginning with an accent or swelling from a soft attack are used for expressive reasons and are often indicated by the composer. The basic attack, however, is one in which the tone begins and continues at the same dynamic level.

MULTIPLE ARTICULATION

Passages requiring the use of the tongue, when too rapid for the single tongue described above, may be articulated by using one of several multiple tonguing techniques. If the passage in question contains notes in groups of two, or multiples of two, the flutist normally resorts to the so-called double tongue.

Here, the articulation is accomplished by alternating the tip of the tongue, as in the basic single tongue, with a point further back on the tongue, as in the consonant *k*. This will usually result in a pattern similar to *tah-kah*, in the effort also to keep the throat open.

Some students will find the softer syllables *duh-guh*, easier to produce, and should be encouraged to concentrate on whichever articulation proves more rewarding. In later study, both of these articulations are used; the *tah-kah* is somewhat sharper in response, and the *duh-guh* is a softer, and often faster, articulation.

As in studying the single tongue, the student should begin in the middle register with slow, repeated tones, proceed diatonically up or down, then return to the middle octave, and continue in the opposite direction. Gradually, the repeated tones should be accelerated, then followed by groups of four notes, then two notes on each pitch, and finally the double tongue should be applied to scale and arpeggio studies.

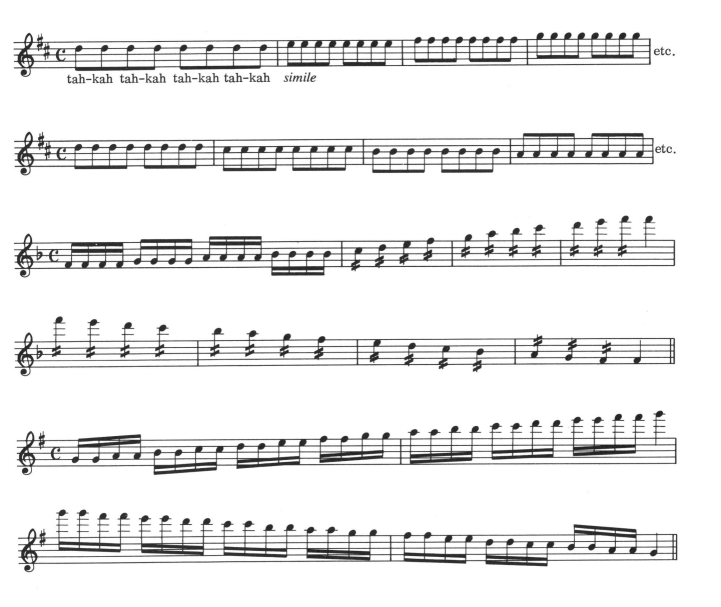

Particular effort must be directed toward evenness of the two syllables, both rhythmically and dynamically. For this reason, slow study is essential in the beginning, with emphasis upon maintaining an open throat, soft articulation, and relaxed tongue. Practicing these studies with the syllable pattern reversed, as shown below, will significantly help develop the necessary evenness in the double tongue.

Rapidly tongued notes that divide into groups of three are normally tongued with one of the varieties of triple tongue. The student is advised to study all three types illustrated, with emphasis upon the third. The first, *tkt-tkt,* is quite commonly used, but tends to be uneven because of the two *t*'s in succession.

The second, *tdk-tdk,* can be quite satisfactory, but many flutists will find it too difficult to master. The *d* articulation on the second note of each triplet is the same as the rolled *r* of the Latin languages, and often is best explained to the student in this way. This is also, consequently, referred to in some texts as *trk,* and can be misleading to English-speaking peoples.

The third type of triple tongue illustrated is the one most used by flutists, and the one most highly recommended. The basic technique is the same as that of the double tongue—the alternation of *t-k* or *d-g* syllables — and thus tends to be more even. It also is of advantage in odd groups of five or seven notes: the flutist is not concerned with the starting or ending syllable, simply alternating them as needed.

Since this type of multiple tongue is often hard for the beginner to control, it is again necessary to start with very slow, deliberate practice on one tone, then proceed as outlined above, but in groups of threes or fives, and so on.

CHAPTER V

BREATH CONTROL

PRINCIPAL TECHNIQUES

The pedagogy of breath control is treated in detail on pages 22-24. Let it suffice here to stress the importance of the two principal factors in proper breathing for the flutist: sufficient quantity of air, and adequately controlled pressure or support to ensure a steady air stream.

The only satisfactory, and perhaps possible, means of achieving these is through exploiting the diaphragm and the abdominal muscles. Simply stated, the diaphragm is a muscular membrane extending horizontally across the torso and separating the chest and abdominal cavities.

Although the abdominal muscles principally control the action needed, we usually speak of the process as diaphragmatic breathing, in contrast to chest breathing. Breathing with the abdomen as well as the chest enables the flutist, first, to produce a steady pressure or support for the air column. Though great pressure in flute playing is not required, steady controlled pressure is.

Lacking resistance to the air stream, except the small amount afforded by the lips themselves, the steady pressure essential to an evenly sustained tone needs the delicate and reliable control available only through using the abdominal muscles.

Some additional control is afforded by use of the chest muscles, but although a valuable asset, this should not be emphasized to beginning students, for it encourages either a tightening of the abdomen, preventing the use of this area, or an overuse of the chest in breathing.

Second, the diaphragm enables the flutist to realize the full capacity of his lungs by allowing them to expand downward into the abdominal cavity as well as outward within the chest cavity, or rib cage. This latter area when used exclusively is too limited to permit enough air to be inhaled.

To impress the significance of quantity of air and related importance of the diaphragm on the flutist, say that ideally he needs a gigantic pair of lungs wholly out of human proportions; so the least he can do is to utilize to the utmost the capabilities he does have! The student will also do well to remember that, in striving for a big, brilliant sound, he will only get out of the flute what he puts into it.

BASIC PHRASING

To avoid confusion in terminology, we should point out that wind instrument players use the term *phrase* in two ways: referring to the musical phrase as an aspect of form, and referring to the act of taking a breath. Although the flutist most commonly breathes in accordance with the musical phrase, often he must breathe more frequently, and at times even play several phrases in one breath.

The beginning student should be encouraged to mark the places for his breath and observe the marks as soon as possible in his study. Generally, the following principles should be observed in determining where to breathe:

1. In accordance with the musical phrase, where practical.

Laura Lee

Moderato

S. Foster

2. In rests, when available, but not in every one if the music consists of many small fragments.

Sonata in B♭ Major

Largo

G. P. Telemann

3. Breathing when rests are not available depends upon stealing time from the previous note, and therefore should be after the longest note available.

Sonata in E Minor

Affettuoso

G. P. Telemann

4. It is better to break a slur (not a tie) than to break the rhythm.

Concertino

Moderato

C. Chaminade

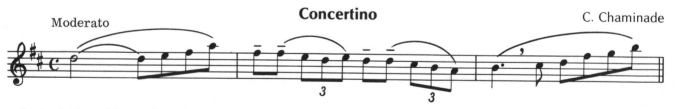

5. Avoid breathing before the last note or two of a phrase, even though they may be preceded by the longest note in the phrase.

In addition, the beginning student must not be allowed to get in the habit of breathing before each note that is tongued: this is an extremely difficult habit to overcome later. Take particular care with the beginnings and endings of phrases to avoid: (1) the tendency to breathe only on bar lines, ignoring pickups; (2) the tendency to accent the ends of phrases.

The second effect is sometimes caused simply by expelling the air that is left over, causing a dynamic push at the end of the phrase. Or it may be an extra action of the tongue in cutting off the note with a *tut* rather than simply stopping the air.

VIBRATO

Since the basic tone of the flute is relatively pure, in terms of lack of overtones, the use of vibrato is particularly desirable to add interest as well as expressiveness to the tone. There are several means of producing a vibrato in flute playing, although they are by no means equally desirable. The necessary pulsations in tone may be achieved by movement of the jaw or lips, by contractions of the throat, or by variations in the intensity of the air stream.

Vibrato produced by moving the lips or the jaw is not normally desirable because it disturbs the embouchure, is too difficult to control in both speed and amplitude, and is often so wide a pitch variant that it seriously disturbs intonation.

Vibrato originating in the throat is most often the natural vibrato produced unconsciously by students. Considerable variety in this type of vibrato is found among students, but it is seldom satisfactory. Throat vibratos are generally too fast, too wide, too uneven, and tend to cause undesirable throat tension. This type of vibrato can rarely be varied in speed and, at best, has a limited application.

Nearly always superior is the type of vibrato dependent on changes in the relative intensity of the air stream. This is usually referred to as a diaphragm vibrato, although this description is not quite accurate, for it is usually produced by using the rib, or intercostal, muscles.

By making the pulsations of the vibrato dependent primarily on dynamic or intensity changes rather than variations in pitch, the flutist may avoid disturbing intonation. This type of vibrato also lends itself more successfully to the demands of musical expression, since it affords a wide range of control in both speed or frequency, and in width or amplitude.

Developing the control of this type of vibrato, fortunately, is not nearly so difficult as one might judge. The student first practices sustaining a pitch in the middle register, such as C^2, with as unfluctuating a sound as possible. This should be at a comfortable dynamic level, and without crescendo or diminuendo.

He next adds a slow, exaggerated pulse, similar to a *ha-ha,* produced primarily with the abdominal muscles, at about $\quad = 72$. At this point, the pulses must be exaggerated to ensure developing control, and the air must be sustained between pulses.

Continuing development is concerned with speeding up the pulses until a musically usable speed is achieved. This will be about five or six cycles per second, or sixteenth notes at the rate of $\quad = 72+$. The study should then be extended to the upper and lower registers, and then relaxed in dynamic amplitude when evenness and control are acquired.

The instructor is cautioned not to begin a student's study of vibrato until his embouchure is reasonably well developed. These studies can confuse the issue if started before a good basic sound has been established. If the beginner has a not-too-obnoxious natural vibrato, leave well enough alone until later. If the student produces an amusical throat quiver, or similar distraction, have him concentrate on producing a straight, even sound, and on correct breathing and support of tone.

As the student increases the speed of his vibrato, the rib muscles will come into play and basically control the pulsation. When his vibrato approaches a usable speed, he will feel the pulse more in his throat, but this is not to be confused with the throat vibrato discussed previously.

CHAPTER VI

BEGINNING INSTRUCTION

SEQUENCE AND TECHNIQUE

The initial concern of the student will be to produce a sound, any sound, on the instrument. Often this is best accomplished by first using only the head joint of the flute rather than the entire instrument, although there is no reason to separate these steps when the student is immediately capable of producing a tone.

With the example of the instructor's demonstration, the aid of practice before a mirror, and the instructor's coaching, the student should shortly be rewarded with the consistent production of tone on the head joint. Progressing to the assembled flute, the student should be carefully advised in the correct alignment of its three sections.

Beginning his first experiences with whole notes and half notes, the student should be reminded as often as necessary to hold his flute with his head up and his arms free of his body, and to support the flute correctly: with thumb and little finger in the right hand, plus the base of the left forefinger.

The student should also be encouraged to stand while practicing, as well as during lessons, to facilitate proper breathing.

It is also during this earliest period of study that the student should be instructed in the basic attack. Refinements of attack may come later, but the habit of starting tones without using the tongue is definitely to be avoided. This bad habit is extremely hard to correct later, but requires a minimum of effort to avoid at this stage.

The student next begins the struggle to learn the fingerings of the flute, together with the many aspects of rhythm, notation, etc. Most method books, though basically well planned, progress too rapidly for the flute student who has had no previous musical training.

Besides the task of developing the embouchure, attack, finger technique, and proper hand and arm position, the student is faced with learning the many features of music notation and applying this to the flute.

Of great aid to the student at this point is the use of supplementary material to allow each item of new knowledge and skill to be thoroughly assimilated and applied. Fortunately, there are a number of very easy collections of folk and popular music for flute, in both solo and duet form. These require knowledge of only two or three accidentals and cover a range of two octaves or less.

These materials should be introduced as soon as the student is able to attempt them. They are invaluable for the interest they encourage, and for the opportunity they afford to assimilate and use knowledge and abilities as they are attained.

Also, most method books are inclined to take the student down to the lowest C on the flute almost immediately. This is unwise; the vast majority of students have great difficulty at first in producing the lowest tones on the instrument.

Again, until a more satisfactory method is available, supplementary exercises avoiding these low tones will help. So will some extra patience on the part of the instructor, plus the explanation that the student cannot really be expected immediately to produce a satisfactory sound on these bottom tones.

It should also be understood that the pads on most school flutes do not seat well enough to give the student an even break on these low notes.

As soon as the student begins playing in the second octave, work on the use of the jaw should also begin. In many cases, this study will be necessary before the student is able to attain a sound in the second octave, or in the bottom octave if his basic embouchure naturally produces the first overtone.

The concept of correct jaw movement is usually acquired by the student after a demonstration by his instructor. Occasionally, the student will have some problems in duplicating this jaw action, because he will be using muscles that he may not have consciously controlled before.

The student will normally be aided by changing the relationship of the lower incisors to the upper. In the average overbite, the lower front teeth are slightly behind the upper ones. Without holding the flute, the student is instructed to bring the lower teeth forward until they are even with the upper teeth, then in front of them, and back again, until he realizes the action of the jaw that is essential in flute playing.

Practice in front of a mirror, with or without the flute, is also recommended. Often the concept of blowing more across the flute, or down into it, or of moving the lower lip in or out as the case may require, will also help the student to accomplish the proper jaw movement.

To develop this use of the jaw, one should depend principally on the study of long tones and octaves, as follows:

These long tones should begin on a central tone, such as C^2, descend diatonically in any key, return to the starting tone, then ascend diatonically for one to one and a half octaves. To control pitch and tone, the jaw is pulled back (but not down) in crescendo, and brought forward in diminuendo.

The sustained tones should be practiced with as much dynamic variation as possible, and be sustained as long as possible. In early studies, the movement of the jaw is best exaggerated. If the tone occasionally breaks in crescendo or disappears or drops an octave in decrescendo, well and good!

It is only by allowing this to occur that the flutist learns just where the tone will break or disappear, and can subsequently control it with confidence. Constant attention to intonation in these studies will serve as the guide in determining the exact amount of movement needed by the jaw.

Suppose the student's natural embouchure produces a tone that is unusually loud, or he has difficulty in supporting tone in the second octave, or he naturally plays with the jaw quite far back. Then he should begin this study by starting long tones forte and concentrating only on the extended diminuendo, while bringing the jaw forward and listening to the pitch as a guide. When this feature of control is satisfactorily attained, he may proceed to the study of both the crescendo and diminuendo, as outlined above.

If a student naturally plays with the jaw unusually extended, he should take the opposite approach. Long tone study may begin with a soft attack, followed by an exaggerated crescendo. The emphasis on pulling the jaw back and blowing down into the flute, without dipping the head, is to be combined with the effort to keep the pitch even.

In the study of octaves to aid in learning the use of the jaw, the student should also begin in the middle range, such as A^1 and A^2. From here he may proceed either diatonically or chromatically downward, return to the starting tone, and then proceed upward in the same manner.

These steps are best practiced very slowly and deliberately, with emphasis on gradually increasing intensity in preparation for the upper tone, rather than lurching up to it by means of a sudden increase of air pressure. The jaw movement should generally be exaggerated until the student is aware of the precise changes in breath support, lips, and jaw needed for octave control.

In some instances, when the difficulty lies in pulling the jaw back enough to control the low octave, it may be best to invert this study. Beginning with the upper tone softly, the student slurs down with crescendo and returns, as illustrated:

Also note that the corners of the mouth will be drawn back more for the lower tones and relaxed forward for the upper ones, as will be encouraged by the jaw movement.

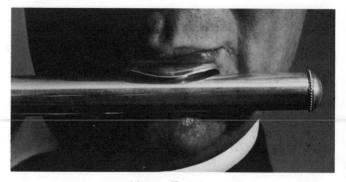

Lower Tones

Upper Tones

The student, meanwhile, through continued progress in his method book, is acquiring the chromatic fingerings of the first few keys beyond C major. As before, extra help in the form of supplementary melodic exercises is invaluable for most beginners. When the student is reasonably familiar with the fingerings for the first few accidentals, he is ready to begin the study of scales —at this stage as an aid to embouchure development rather than for finger technique.

One of the most satisfactory approaches to beginning scale study is as follows:

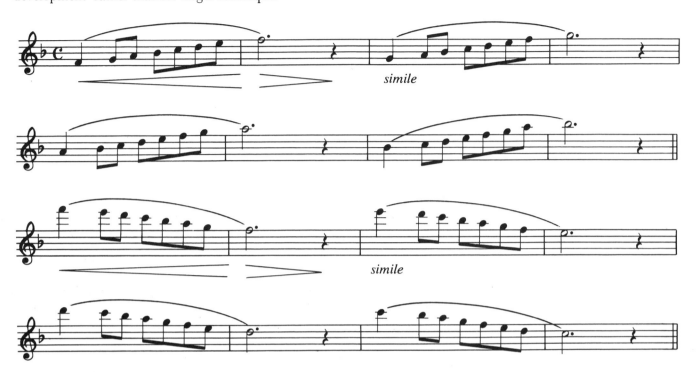

simile

simile

The student should begin the pattern only as low as is feasible for himself, and only progress as high as it proves convenient, not necessarily either beginning or ending on the tonic pitch. It is better to practice these scales without reading the notes, but if a student finds this too difficult at first, he may write the pattern out for each scale and read it until he becomes able to dispense with the written version.

This study is intended as an aid in developing both the embouchure and finger technique, so the following points should be stressed:

1. To improve tonal quality throughout the range of the flute, the student extends the sound only one note at a time with each measure—into the upper register when ascending, and down into the bottom range when descending.

2. The notes should be played as smoothly legato, and as even in both rhythm and tone as the student can manage. Legato is recommended to reveal the interpolated notes that result from uneven fingering.

3. The student is to practice the notes slowly enough so that fingering is not a serious problem, but correct basic fingering must be used without exception.

4. To aid in developing breath control, air should be taken only in the rests. If the student has trouble in playing the entire octave in one breath, the tempo may be accelerated.

5. For progressive difficulty in key sequence, scales would be studied in keys of increasing sharps and flats rather than a strict circle of fourths or fifths.

The recommended sequence of major scales thus would be F, G, Bb, D, etc.

You will also discover that these scales, when practiced without reading the notes, will significantly aid the student in becoming conscious of tones and pitches, rather than the all-too-common tendency to think only in terms of symbols and related fingerings. Many of the later problems of coordination can be averted at this time by making the student sufficiently conscious of the relationship of note symbol, letter name, fingering, and sound.

The beginning student, however, can hardly be expected to remember all of these when they have been mentioned only once or twice in his flute method. Much additional drill is desirable and, fortunately, can easily be provided. Scale study, as discussed above, encourages the student to relate sounds, symbols, and fingerings.

To aid in learning the symbols apart from the fingerings, it is usually sufficient to have the student write the note names above or below his studies until he attains some proficiency. Next, he is required to name the notes verbally during the lesson period and later to sing his exercises in a convenient octave, with the note names. The value of sight-singing and solfege cannot be emphasized enough, and all possible effort should be made in this type of study.

The balance of instruction for the beginning student will be a continuation of the basic principles already considered. Given a good approach to the correct hand and arm position, finger technique will develop rapidly as the student progresses through his study materials. Some additional work on the fingerings involving independence of the ring fingers, is advisable, however, such as:

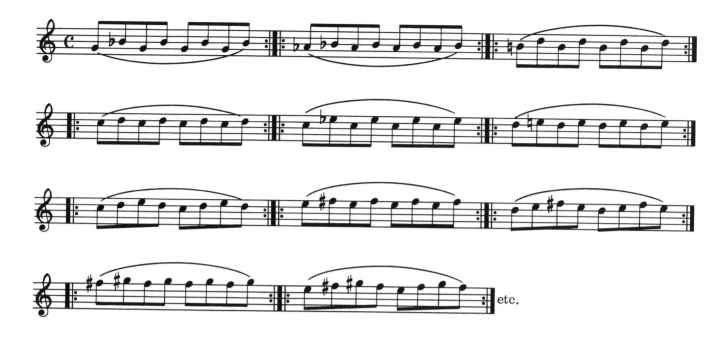

Extra practice is also recommended on all fingerings in the highest octave. For the present, this need only be additional time spent on the scale studies in this range.

Developing the embouchure is a matter of constant refinement of the basic lip formation and jaw action. The greatest aids in this direction are found in the study of scales, long tones, and octaves, as outlined above. The student at this stage should normally strive for the biggest sound he can manage. Refinements of this tone are relatively easy to develop once this basic sound is established.

Breath control is also to be improved in this intermediate period of study. For the student who does not have difficulty in using the full capacity of his abdominal and chest cavities, this is largely a matter of correct phrasing.

He should be constantly encouraged to use the largest quantity of air possible in producing a tone, and instructed in the proper places in which to take his breaths. Long tones are sustained as long as possible and scales are studied in strict tempo, so that the student must take enough breath in a very short period of time.

In his other studies, the student must take care not to break the rhythm or phrase with his breaths, and is encouraged to mark breaths in his studies with a √ or '. In this manner, good habits may be formed at this early period of learning that will become necessities in performance. The student should approach any study as if it is a significant piece of music literature. Playing or practicing indifferently is a waste of time!

CORRECTING COMMON PROBLEMS

The problems most often met by students of the flute are those concerned with the embouchure. These are usually the result of physical characteristics of the lip greatly divergent from the norm, or a lack of muscular control in forming and using an effective embouchure, or in the use of the jaw.

Just as all other physical characteristics vary from person to person, so too lip structures vary in both shape and size. Although it is commonly accepted that persons with thin lips will be ideally suited for the flute, there is in reality no ideal in this regard. The important factors, rather, are the amount of the embouchure hole that is covered by the lower lip, and the shape and direction of the air stream.

In most cases, correct placement of the embouchure hole will be accomplished by placing its near edge on the edge of the lower lip: the line formed by the lower edge of the red, fleshy part of the lip. If the student's lower lip is unusually thick, the edge of the embouchure hole should be moved up slightly on the lip, to cover less of the hole.

In case the student's lip is unusually thin, he must cover slightly more of the hole by moving the flute down below the edge of the lower lip. You realize, of course, that a relatively small fraction of an inch is a large change in so delicate an adjustment.

In making changes of this nature, it is well to remember that a compensating change in the angle of the flute will usually also be needed. The flute may be turned in or out slightly until the correct angle for the air stream is reestablished.

The relation between the thickness of the upper lip and the lower lip may also cause difficulty in producing sound by affecting the direction of the air stream. An upper lip that is unusually thick or fleshy in relation to the lower lip will cause the student to blow down too directly into the flute. This may generally be corrected by changing the relative tension of the lips.

The corners of the mouth are drawn back, or even down, to make the upper lip firmer while allowing the lower lip to remain relatively fleshy. If this proves insufficient, further adjustment is necessary by bringing the lower jaw forward and, consequently, the lower lip.

In the opposite instance, when the upper lip is so thin in relation to the lower one that the student normally blows across the embouchure plate at too slight an angle, improvement can be made by bringing the corners of the mouth up slightly to flatten the lower lip against the teeth and drawing back the jaw.

Since the upper lip must at all times cover the upper front teeth, some students will find it necessary to pull the lip down over the teeth in cases wherein the lip normally allows the upper teeth to protrude. This type of extreme overbite will usually also require the average position of the lower jaw to be quite far forward.

In addition to these considerations, the shape of the student's lips in forming an aperture may cause problems in centering the air stream. Thicker portions on either the upper or lower lip will often produce apertures resembling the following, rather than the norm:

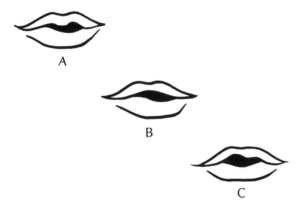

A

B

C

Note that in Example B above, the off-center embouchure is usually caused by pushing the flute to the player's left, rather than by a physical characteristic of the lips. In any case, the solution is to move the lower lip to the right or left as needed and approximate the desired aperture formation.

Occasionally, a thickness of the upper lip in the center may produce a "split embouchure," such as:

The solution of this problem is usually to move the lower lip to the right or left, and match one of the apertures in the upper lip with the natural aperture in the lower lip. The student may also have to learn to close the other aperture by pressing the lips together on that side.

Practice before a mirror is invaluable in establishing any of these embouchure changes. The use of long tone studies is basic here, along with slow scale practice after the new embouchure is reasonably well formed.

Problems arising from unusual jaw relationships are generally less difficult to overcome. In the rather common overbite, the average position of the lower jaw may easily be adjusted to one in which the jaw starts already somewhat forward in the lowest range.

When the lower jaw is generally too far forward, the position of the flute on the lip, and its angle, will need to be shifted in. The student must then practice pulling the jaw back while forcing the tone in the low octave, also stretching the lower lip and flattening it against the teeth by pulling the corners of the mouth back considerably.

In all of these problems involving the embouchure or jaw, the instructor is advised to use the sound as his guide. The tonal quality will be the most reliable clue to a student's difficulties.

If the tone is unusually thin or small, the student is covering too much of the embouchure hole. This may be the result of lip placement, turning the flute in too far, the shape of the lips, or the position of the jaw. The correction is made by moving the edge of the embouchure hole up on the lip and/or bringing the jaw forward, plus readjusting the angle of the flute.

When the tone is too shallow or empty, the student is generally covering too little of the embouchure hole. This may be corrected by simply covering more hole with the lower lip, or turning the flute in slightly, or pulling the jaw back, or by a combination of these changes.

Remember, the essential problem here is not blowing down into the flute enough or not covering enough hole, and this comment alone will often be all the advice the student needs.

Remember also that the degree that the flute is turned in or out depends primarily on the amount of embouchure hole covered by the lip, and the direction of the air stream normally produced by the student. In correcting any basic embouchure problem, it is well to experiment a moment to determine the correct amount that the flute should be turned in or out. This can easily be heard, for the tone will disappear entirely at both extremes, and somewhere in the middle the best sound possible for the moment should be immediately apparent.

Windiness of tone may be the result of any one of several problems, but in each case it is because too much of the air stream is striking the sides of the embouchure hole. When this breathiness is accompanied by a very shallow, empty, or bland quality of sound, it is most often caused by blowing across the flute at too slight an angle, or by too large an aperture in the lips.

More often, however, wind in the tone is caused by air striking one of the sides of the embouchure hole. This may be the result of an unusually shaped lip aperture or incorrect centering of the air column. Normally, the aperture in the lips can be seen by the instructor and centered with no great difficulty.

To check the center of the air column in questionable instances, the embouchure plate should be thoroughly cleaned. Then the condensation of moisture on the plate, while the student plays, will accurately reveal the placement of the air stream.

The student may have difficulty in controlling the first two octaves of the flute's range (in which the sound continually drops down to the fundamental octave, or the student plays both octaves when attempting to play the upper). In that case he should bring the lower jaw forward along with the lower lip to cover more hole and, at first, to increase his breath support when playing in the second octave.

This can then be improved by the study of slow octave slurs and slow ascending scales, as discussed above. The student having difficulty in controlling either of the extreme octaves should also concentrate on slow scale studies. The principal problem is not enough use of the jaw, and the range must be gradually extended in the desired direction.

A student's problems involving support of the flute or fingering are usually the result of incorrect hand position. If the physical problem seems to be one of coordination, it is usually the result of a lack of independence in the ring, or third, finger of the right hand, or occasionally of both hands. Additional study similar to the following examples will be most rewarding:

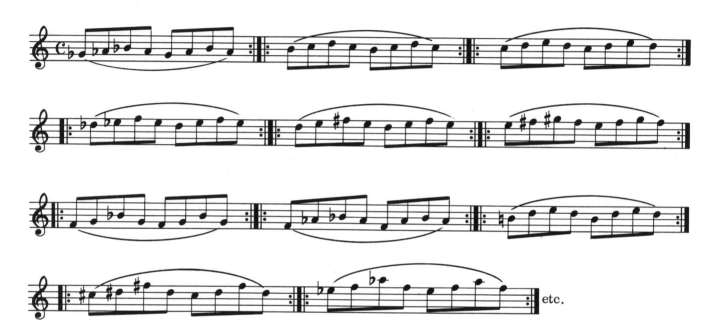

These are to be practiced very slowly at first, using only the basic fingerings. The studies are then gradually speeded up, but the fingers must remain relaxed and consciously controlled. As soon as the fingers tighten or become tense, the student must pause, slow down the tempo, and start again.

Occasionally a student's difficulties are the result of pressing so rigidly with the fingers that their joints collapse and lock. Obviously, any finger dexterity is impossible to attain in this manner, and the student should again concentrate on slow scale practice and finger exercises, such as the above. In these, he must concentrate on light and relaxed finger action, with the tips of the fingers in the key-cups.

Another problem often retarding the progress of beginning flute students is the neglect of the diaphragm in breath control and support. In most cases, the student will be encouraged to develop and exploit the possibilities of the diaphragm if he is simply instructed to keep striving for longer and longer phrases in all of his study, and to take the largest breaths possible in the shortest space of time.

The student who still has difficulty in fully utilizing the capacities of his breathing aparatus must first be made conscious of what it entails. Discussion and demonstration of the distinctions between breathing primarily in the chest cavity and breathing primarily with the aid of the abdominal muscles are most helpful, and often all that is necessary. Of additional aid to the student are:

1. Instruction to keep the throat as open as possible when inhaling, in order to take in a greater quantity of air.

2. Blowing as hard as possible on some object, such as the thumb, inserted in the mouth, to make the student conscious of the pressure that can be exerted by the muscles in both the lower abdomen and the chest.

3. An exaggerated laugh, or a cough, which also demonstrate the sensation of using these muscles.

4. Relaxing the abdominal muscles to allow use of the diaphragm in posture-conscious youths who are constantly pulling in the stomach and expanding the chest. Good posture is important in flute playing, but exaggerated muscle tension is not necessary to correct posture, and will certainly hamper correct breathing.

5. The realization that breathing mainly in the chest

cavity is not as natural as breathing with the diaphragm. When one is most relaxed, as in sleep, he will breathe in the more desirable fashion.

6. Pulling in the abdomen or raising the shoulders when inhaling are both clues to incorrect breathing.

7. Controlled support in breathing is best developed through the practice of dynamically even long tones, in which the tone is sustained as long as possible at the same intensity.

SOME ADDITIONAL PRECAUTIONS

Many of the handicaps that students have in the course of their flute study are the direct result of bad habits assimilated, often as short cuts, during the earliest periods of their training. Since these habits are so easy to fall into (and sometimes even recommended by instructors and method books), every effort should be made to form good habits in their stead at the earliest opportunity.

One of the commonest pitfalls is the tendency to cover too much of the embouchure hole with the lower lip. This may be the result of placing the flute too far down on the chin, or turning the flute in too far. It is a very tempting habit, for a relatively pretty sound may be produced in this manner with a minimum of effort. The student, however, will find it impossible to develop beyond the consequent small, thin tone. Lip facility in controlling slurred intervals will be wanting, and the instrument cannot respond readily to attack, often resulting in a disagreeable delay between the sound of the attack and the tone itself.

This is also a tempting habit because it requires relatively little air to produce a tone. But laziness here denies any further development of tone or facility.

An additional problem worth attention is the tendency to break the phrase or even the rhythm for too frequent breaths. The student is in most cases simply taking the easy way out and, rather than inhaling enough air in premarked phrases, stops continually for breath with little or no regard for the phrase or the rhythm.

In addition to the obvious amusical habit being formed, the student is seriously postponing development of proper breath control. To correct this demands that phrases be marked and observed at all times.

Sometimes, frequent breaths are an excuse to gain time in preparation for a technically difficult passage. This may be recognized when the student breaks the rhythm for his breath by hesitating before a difficult passage, although he may not be in need of air at all. He will stop, take a breath, get set, and continue.

This is the result of a habit set in practice, and it will be noted that the student always makes the breaks in the same places and always just before a troublesome passage. This is not a dishonest attempt to fool his instructor, but a completely natural reaction to technical difficulties. The student stumbles over a troublesesome passage in his study, and the hesitant stop soon becomes habitual.

Fortunately, this habit, once recognized, is easily corrected. The student is instructed to work out the difficult spot slowly and to play through the break until he is familiar enough with it to phrase properly.

In the study of attack, the student must exercise care to avoid the easy habit of letting the tongue protrude between the lips. This interferes considerably with the embouchure, and causes an unpleasant sound of attack to precede the actual tone. Sometimes the student also forms the habit of cutting off tones with the tongue rather than allowing them to cease naturally by interrupting the air supply. Although both of these techniques are occasionally used, they are not recommended as a basic attack for the beginner.

Occasionally, beginners acquire an extremely bad habit that is almost impossible to correct later. In seeking support for the embouchure, the student may anchor the tongue behind the lower teeth and use the middle portion of the tongue for articulation. Or, even worse, he may support the lower lip with the tongue and use the throat (*kah*) for articulation. Musically, these are impossible concepts, and completely prevent the flutist's progress beyond the beginning level. When detected, this practice should immediately be discouraged, even to the extent of returning the student to the exclusive practice of slow sustained tones and the basic attack.

In trying to develop finger dexterity, there are several bad habits that can hamper the student because they seem like easy shortcuts at first, but they soon prove to be handicaps to better playing. The importance of correct hand position must be reemphasized here: any great variation will prevent the development of all but the most rudimentary technical skill.

By far the most serious and common pitfall for beginning students is the use of alternate fingerings before thoroughly learning the basic ones. Because of the poor quality and intonation of all alternate fingerings, the student soon faces the task of undoing the fingering habits he has formed and acquiring the correct habits in their stead. The process is as inevitable as it is difficult, the shortcut having now become a setback. Some of these fingering problems are met so often that they deserve specific mention.

Probably the commonest troublemaker in fingering is the incorrect use of the Bb lever activated by the left thumb. This thumb key is used for ease of fingering in countless instances, but it is an aid to finger dexterity and must not be allowed to become a hindrance instead.

The student should begin his studies by using only the basic fingering for Bb, even though this will at times prove more difficult than the thumb key. Only after the student has firmly established the habit of using the basic fingering should he be introduced to this thumb key. Then he will shortly be capable of discovering its values, as well as problems, for himself.

If the student is introduced to the thumb key too soon in his study, he will form the habit of using it constantly for B♭ and consequently often be forced to slide or roll his thumb between the two keys. To the beginner this may seem to present no problem, but he will soon be handicapped because there is a definite limitation to the speed and ease with which the thumb can slide. In addition, the teacher (if not the student) will soon be disturbed to discover the student often playing B♭ when B♮ is the composer's intention.

The student who has already succumbed to this unfortunate habit will find it necessary to force himself to use the basic fingering consistently in his studies. He will need to do this, even though it is more difficult than using the thumb key. When he has mastered its use, both fingerings can be used to advantage.

Care must also be taken to develop correct fingering of the first three octaves of D and D♯. These basic fingerings are essential to control the octaves, as well as for better intonation and quality. The beginning student is often not conscious of these differences and tends to use the easiest fingering: that is, the same for all three octaves.

Again, little effort is required to establish the correct fingerings at the start. But considerable time and effort will be spent in correcting fingerings later.

Another common error is the use of the alternate fingering for F♯, often in passages that are not difficult, even to the exclusion of the correct fingering. The quality of tone produced by this alternate fingering is considerably inferior to the basic F♯, although it may not be apparent to the novice. The student who is acquainted with it too soon may use this alternate fingering at all times.

True, this fingering does facilitate a few difficult passages and is used in the E-F♯ trill, but this need be of no concern to the beginner. The student must form the habit of using the correct F♯ fingering for the sake of developing independence between the third and fourth fingers of the right hand. It also results in better tone and intonation.

One may generalize by saying that teaching any alternate fingering before the basic fingerings are firmly established in the student's mind is to be strenuously avoided.

A notorious practice is the teaching of alternate fingerings for the high octave, or advocating the use of harmonics to facilitate finger technique. Quality and intonation are obviously sacrificed, but the student's embouchure development is also retarded, since he is forced to overblow to produce most of these harmonics or other alternates.

In every instance, the student and/or instructor grasps at the knowledge of alternate fingerings as a panacea for lack of facility, only to discover that he has, instead, placed a stumbling block in the path of acquiring that very facility.

In summing up these basic points for the beginner, the following checklist is intended as an aid to both student and instructor. These reminders are to be referred to continually until a good basic approach to flute playing has been established, then only somewhat less often in striving for perfection.

1. *Alignment:* Embouchure hole in line with C♯ key; rod of foot joint in line with center of D key.

2. *Position of Arms:* Flute held almost horizontally; elbows away from body; head up.

3. *Hand Position:* Flute supported by base of left forefinger; right thumb under first and second fingers, and right little finger. Fingers curved, with tips resting lightly on the keys.

4. *Embouchure:* Check centering, angle of flute, amount of hole covered, and jaw position. Listen! Can the tone be improved?

5. *Fingering:* Correct basic fingerings for B♭, D, D♯, F♯; all of the high register should be used. Right little finger should be depressed when called for.

6. *Attack:* Tongue must not protrude unnecessarily, cut off tones, or be anchored behind lower lip. Syllable *tah* is to be used in basic articulation.

7. *Breath Control:* Full capacity of the lungs and steady, sufficient breath support realized through use of both abdominal and chest cavities. Phrase without interrupting musical thought or rhythm.

8. *The Instrument:* Occasionally check the position of the stopper in the head joint, as well as the general mechanical condition of the flute.

BASIC FINGERING CHART

Key

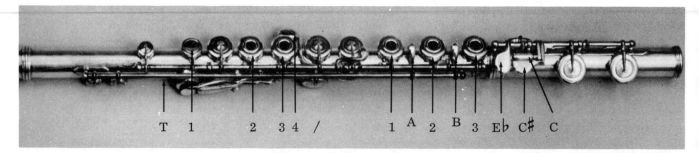

T   1   2   3 4 /   1 A 2 B 3 E♭ C♯ C

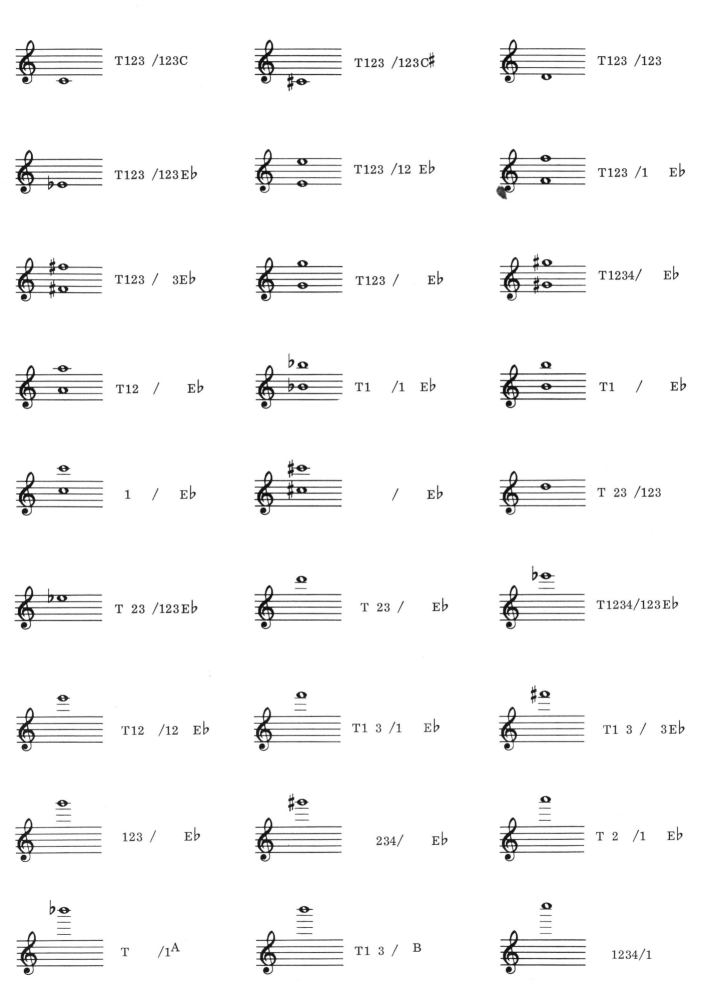

27

To establish the use of the correct basic fingering for the D's and D♯'s, and to understand the relationship of all fingerings in the third octave to the lower ones, the exercise below should be memorized. It is also valuable in refining intonation and octave control.

ARTIST
PERFORMANCE

PART TWO

CHAPTER VII

TONAL DEVELOPMENT

QUALITY AND VARIETY

A concept of sound, so necessary to fine flute playing, is almost impossible to convey by means of the written word. It is only in a most limited sense that differences in sound may be described, and even then such descriptions will be best understood by those who already have some aural concept of flute tone.

The student who does not have the example of a fine flutist-instructor to follow should refer to the many excellent solo flute recordings that are available, and compare tonal qualities of as many flutists as he can. After he has achieved a basic concept of the possible varieties of flute sound, the literal descriptions of these should have meaning for him.

In producing and controlling tone on the flute, we are concerned primarily with the following aspects of the tone:

1. Relative brilliance, in contrast to dullness, or blandness.
2. Clarity, or pureness of sound, in contrast to breathiness.
3. Size of tone, running the gamut from small or thin, to large, big, full, etc.
4. Capacity for dynamic variation.
5. Facility, or rapidity of response in producing successive tones, either slurred or articulated.
6. Evenness of quality throughout the range of the instrument.

The ideal to strive toward is the most brilliant tone (the source of the carrying or projecting power of the flute) and the largest, clearest tone throughout the range of the instrument, with the greatest possible dynamic variation and facility.

The infinite variations between this ideal and other qualities of tone are almost all used for expressive reasons in performance, but emphasis in study must be on the ideal as described. Other aspects affecting tone production and effects, such as attack, vibrato, and harmonics, are treated separately.

To develop tonal quality to the best of one's ability, it is desirable to understand the manner in which changes in embouchure, placement, jaw, etc., will affect that quality. Basically, variations in tone will depend on:

1. Centering the air column in relation to the embouchure hole. Lateral errors will cause breathiness; blowing up or down too much affects quality and intonation.
2. The amount of embouchure hole covered by the lip. Within certain limitations, the more hole covered by the lip, the more brilliant the quality of tone, although it also becomes smaller, or thinner, and facility in slurring intervals larger than a second is impaired. So are response and dynamic variety. As less hole is covered, the tone becomes bigger, facility and response are improved, and capacity for dynamic variation is increased. The tone, however, becomes more and more dull or empty.
3. Proper breath control and support; necessary to brilliance, facility, dynamics, and control.
4. Use of the jaw to govern embouchure formation, placement, and direction of air column.
5. The formation of the throat and mouth chamber, and relative position of the tongue.

Since several of these principles are incompatible, the flutist must search for a musical compromise that will enable him to realize all of the varieties of sound available to him. When the basic tone quality described above is attained with some degree of consistency and control, the student will have already discovered some of the variations of tone possible.

As musical expression demands, it should be a simple matter to reduce or increase the brilliance in the tone, change its basic quality to a thin or bland sound, make it clear but shallow, and so forth. Add to these possibilities the variants afforded by attack, vibrato, and so forth, and some of the solo capabilities of the flute may become realized.

To understand and develop the basic flute sound and its varieties, the following study will prove most beneficial:

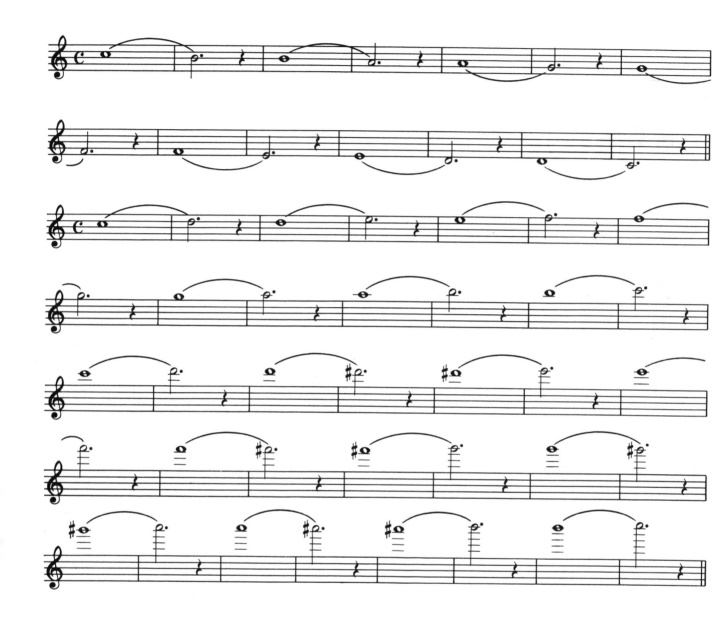

These sustained tones should first be practiced only in mezzo forte, while striving to develop the finest basic sound the student can manage. The tone should be centered, edgy, brilliant, and yet full, not thin. This is accomplished by keeping the throat open as in the vowel sound *ah* throughout the range. Cover about one-fourth to one-third of the embouchure hole with the lower lip in the middle register, somewhat more in ascending, less in descending.

The corners of the mouth should be stretched back somewhat, and the aperture in the lips kept relatively small, while forcing air past them with considerable support. Remember, the lips act like a nozzle on a hose in increasing the intensity of the air column. This creates overtones in the otherwise bland sound of the flute, adding brilliance to the tone.

After this basic sound has been achieved, the student should follow the same routine while mastering the variants of this quality. First, study the bland, dull sound which is produced by covering less embouchure hole, opening the aperture in the lips, and blowing easier. The tendency to play sharp under these circumstances must be countered by drawing the jaw back slightly and taking care not to turn the flute out too much.

Some brilliance may be returned to this type of tone by forcing the air column a bit more without reducing the aperture.

Second, study the varieties of a thinner and more brilliant sound by covering slightly more of the embouchure hole, reducing the aperture in the lips, and forcing the air stream. Take care in this instance to avoid flatting the pitch, by keeping the jaw well forward and, if necessary, turning the flute out slightly.

The third basic factor affecting quality of tone that should be studied is the effect of the various tongue placements. The student should practice these same studies with each of the vowel sounds from the full, open sound of *ah* through the thin quality of the small throat and mouth chamber caused by the *eee* placement.

To refine jaw and embouchure placement further, as well as control pitch, the following exercise will be most rewarding:

etc.

etc.

etc.

etc.

etc.

etc.

34

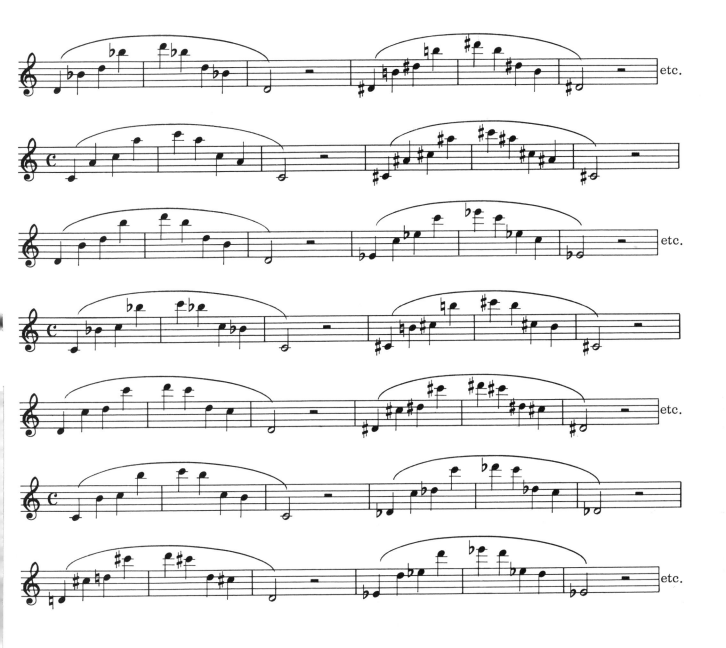

These are to be practiced slowly, with particular attention to intonation, and to smooth, accurate legato connections. In ascending, the increase in breath support must slightly precede the movement of the fingers to avoid a rough legato. It will also help to study these first in mezzo forte, with a slight crescendo in ascending and diminuendo in descending. They should then be practiced in forte and in piano throughout.

Concentration on jaw placement and movement in these studies will lead to sure success, in spite of the advice found in some texts that tightening the embouchure and not moving the chin produces the upper register on the flute.

In summary, control of the range of the flute depends on the following adjustments:

When ascending in range:

1. The jaw comes forward, raising the direction of the air stream.

2. The corners of the lips come in (or forward) to relax the lower lip and cover more embouchure hole.

3. The aperture is smaller and rounder.

4. The lips are more puckered or compressed, less tense, with the lower lip quite fleshy.

5. Breath support increases.

When descending in range:

1. The jaw is pulled back, directing the air column more downward.

2. The corners of the mouth are pulled back, stretching and flattening the lips against the teeth.

3. The aperture becomes larger and more elongated.

4. The lips become tight and firm.

5. Breath support may relax, but air must still be forced through the aperture to maintain intensity and brilliance.

To develop and refine control of intonation and dynamics, as well as tone quality, sustained tones should first be studied as follows:

These should be attacked with the embouchure fairly open, perhaps even in forte. The jaw comes forward in the diminuendo to keep the pitch up, while the lips become more relaxed. Breath support should be lessened while the throat is kept open, as in *ah*.

Sustained tones should next be practiced with both crescendo and diminuendo, to learn the relation between pitch and dynamic levels, as well as their control.

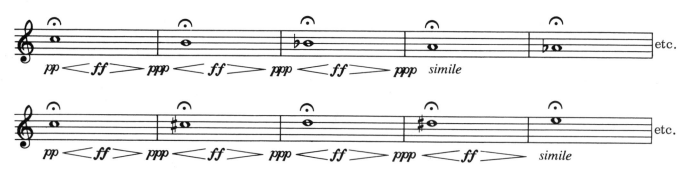

Starting with the jaw forward, the flutist brings it back for the crescendo, and forward again for the diminuendo. The performer will be guided in the amount of jaw movement needed by very carefully maintaining the pitch level throughout each tone. The student will do well to let the tone break periodically in crescendo or disappear in diminuendo, to discover where these extremes lie. In time, this becomes an accurate feeling, so that the flutist may play at either extreme without losing control. He should also remember that he plays softer by blowing less, *not* by pinching the embouchure or by closing the throat.

For further tone development and control in the extreme ranges of the flute, studies similar to the following will encourage rapid improvement.

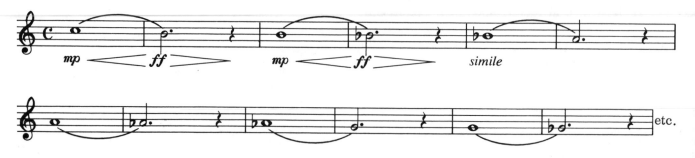

In this low register, emphasis should be on as much crescendo as possible. Again, if the tone breaks at times, this is how the student learns to feel this breaking point and avoid it in performance. Pulling the corners of the mouth back to stretch and flatten the lips should be exaggerated, and the angle of the flute and position of the jaw should be adjusted for optimal tone production.

In many cases, this study will also aid in improving control of the top octave, since loss of control in the upper range is often due to the fact that the student already has his jaw and embouchure too far forward in the low and middle ranges. As he ascends in range, he loses control because he cannot come forward further with his lips and jaw. Emphasizing the extreme position of the jaw and embouchure in the bottom octave makes control of the third octave easier.

A related procedure enables the flutist to improve control of the upper range.

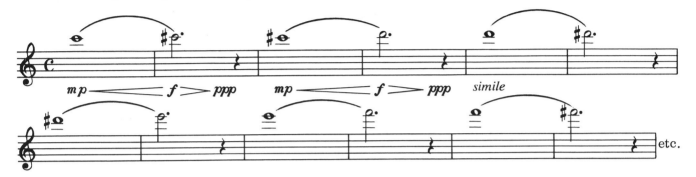

At the end of each tone, the student will do well to feel for the minimum of support necessary for the tone, and perhaps let it disappear and return several times to feel this "threshold of sound." This exercise may also be studied with the dynamic variation noted below, to further refine control of this octave. The student should be conscious of the very slight increase in breath support needed for each semitone.

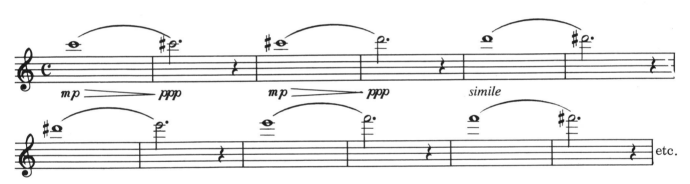

HARMONICS

Although harmonics on the flute are used for several reasons, they are treated here because of their use in tone study. Harmonics are sometimes used as alternate fingerings, as discussed in Chapter IX, and are sometimes called for in literature because of their unusual quality. These are notated in several ways, usually indicating both the pitch to be sounded and the note to be fingered.

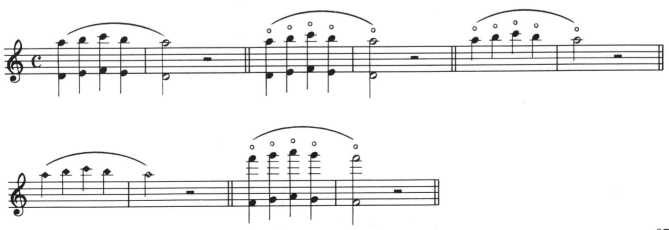

We most commonly use only the first, second, and third harmonics in flute playing, with the first harmonic used for most of the second octave: D^2 to $C\sharp^3$. The second and third harmonics are particularly helpful in developing accurate control of the upper register, when practiced as follows:

In every case, these harmonics are achieved by extending the principles used to sound the second octave of the flute. The jaw is brought forward, the embouchure compressed, and the breath support increased.

The fundamental fingering should change only on the last note of each sequence, and the student should strive for accurate intonation, realizing that the second and third harmonics are considerably flat in pitch. The latter study also helps the student understand his instrument,

in that the upper octave, from $E\flat^3$ through B^3, is based on the fingering of the fundamental octave.

To encourage the sounding of the fourth partial, a different key is opened for each of these tones at about the distance of one-fourth of the effective length of the flute. The compromises necessary in the mechanism can then be seen, to explain the instability of the high E and $F\sharp$, because of the double keys, and of the $G\sharp$, because of the necessity of the small $C\sharp$ hole.

CHAPTER VIII

ARTICULATION

VARIETIES OF THE SINGLE ATTACK

In studying the various types of articulation, the student is reminded of the importance of keeping the air pressure constantly behind the tongue. The breath is stopped between notes only in relatively slow tempos. He should remember that the tongue releases the tone, it does not start it. Also, the tone is stopped by interrupting the air supply, not by cutting it off with the tongue, as in a *tut* articulation. In a series of tongued notes, preparing the tongue for articulation automatically cuts off the previous note.

A softer articulation than the basic *tah* is achieved by using a portion of the tongue behind its tip, as in articulating *doo*. When indicated by the notation, this will usually be in one of the following ways:

All three examples call for the soft tongue, but Example *A*, usually referred to as staccato-legato or mezzo staccato, is slightly spaced between the notes. Examples *B* and *C* are usually played in the same fashion, although the first is called a louré articulation, and the second is a tenuto style. The dashes are referred to as tenuto signs and generally instruct the performer to hold the note its full value. This sign, however, is also used to indicate a dynamic and rhythmic stress or emphasis of a note or notes.

When notes of the same pitch are included under a slur, but not also tied, they are tongued softly.

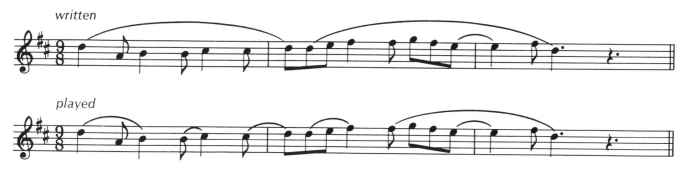

Often confusing in performance is the notation in which only the last note of a group under a slur has a dot over it. In this instance, the last note is shortened but not articulated.

An exception to the above that is probably an error in notation but occurs often enough to warrant mention is the appearance of a dot over the second of two *tied* notes.

Here, the intention must be a soft articulation on the second note, or the dot is meaningless.

Some flutists also recommend a soft articulation, particularly in the upper register, that depends on the syllable *poo* for attack, with the tongue not used at all. Though many flutists have not found this type of attack necessary, it is certainly worthy of trial.

The position of the tongue in the mouth in articulation generally depends on the relative hardness or sharpness of the attack. Bringing the tongue forward, even to touching the teeth, will produce a harder attack, while touching a point further back on the palate will produce a softer attack.

The extremely pointed attack, called *spitzig*, or spitting, in which the tongue actually touches the lips, is sometimes required in literature. This is a very acute, percussive attack, and must be produced with the embouchure open enough so that the tone immediately follows the attack. This tonguing can also be used for an extremely hard attack in the low register of the flute, if enough air pressure is maintained behind the tongue, and the throat is as open as possible.

Note that the practice of slapping one or more keys simultaneously with the attack, to encourage response in the low register, is disturbingly unmusical and also unnecessary for that response. The student may feel more secure with this technique, but the extraneous noise will identify him as an amateur.

The dynamic varieties of these basic single tongue articulations should also be investigated and mastered for their musical possibilities.

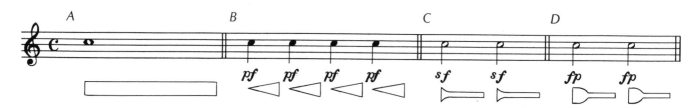

The articulation symbolized in Example A is one in which the attack is at the same dynamic level as the tone that follows, and should be the standard concept of attack. To achieve it, the student may practice scales and arpeggios at moderate speed and at various dynamic levels, with the tongue rather high on the palate to avoid any accent.

Later study with rests between the notes, and equal to them in duration, will develop security and accuracy in this attack.

Example B concerns the soft attack with immediate swell, which rarely is called for in music but is useful in refining control of attack. Example C (often notated by **sf**, **sfz**, **sfp**, or **<**) demands a hard attack, open embouchure and air pressure. To avoid a sudden change in pitch, the attack should begin with the jaw well back, then sustained softly with the jaw brought immediately forward to keep the pitch up.

The forte-piano, diagrammed in Example D above, is also a loud-soft articulation, but with a softer attack. The tongue should be well back on the palate, with the success of the articulation depending on change of air pressure and jaw position.

The study of staccato should begin in slower tempos, with concentration on the action of the tongue and breath supply. In moderate tempos, or on notes of longer values, staccato may be interpreted as shortening the notes to one-half their notated values.

Moderato

The student must be very careful to let the tongue remain free of the palate at the end of each note, and to stop the sound by stopping the air. As speed is gradually increased, the emphasis should be on lightness of articulation, often restricting study at first to the softer dynamics.

In more rapid staccato tonguing, note that preparing the tongue for each attack automatically cuts off the previous tone; cutting tones off with the tongue is uncalled-for and impractical.

MULTIPLE TONGUING

Further refinement of double and triple tonguing may be accomplished by varying the accents, studying the many combinations of slur and tongue patterns, and constantly increasing the speed. Rapid improvement will result from the following studies if the emphasis in their practice is on the equal duration of every note, as well as on speed.

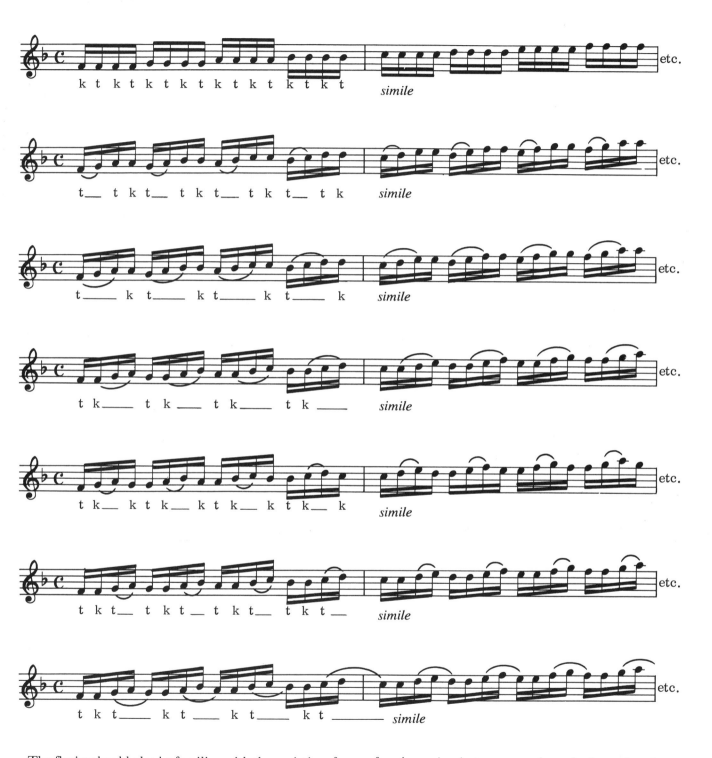

The flutist should also be familiar with the varieties of sound available through the use of the different syllables of articulation. Because of the open throat, *tah-kah* is the preferred approach under most circumstances. A *duh-guh* articulation, however, will usually result in a softer and faster attack, while a *di-ki* or *dee-kee* will produce a thinner sound. This latter is often desirable in softer dynamics, but proves awkward when a heavier or louder sound is needed. Although the exercises above only suggest a *t-k* articulation, all of these varieties should be studied in each pattern.

All of the above principles apply equally to the further development of the triple tongue based on the *t-k-t, k-t-k* articulation, and should be studied separately.

41

Complete control of these multiple articulations will finally be achieved when the flutist can successfully play the more common asymmetrical patterns.

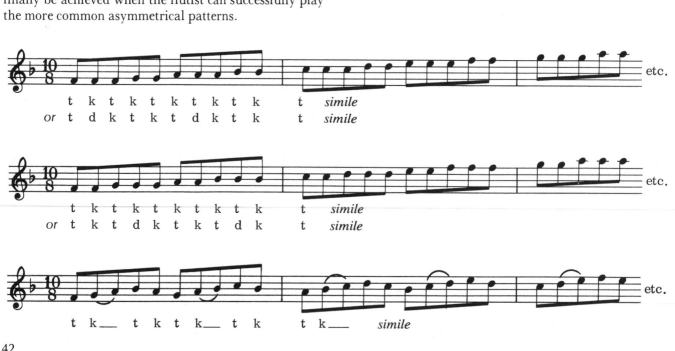

It also helps, in improving multiple articulations, to realize that increased air pressure, or intensity, is necessary to ensure the rapid response of the tones. More intensity of air pressure is needed to tongue notes rapidly than to sustain the same tones at the same dynamic level. As in putting a nozzle on a garden hose, the aperture in the lips must be reduced and the support increased, relative to the pitch and dynamic level.

Note also that multiple tonguing is only used when the notes are too fast to be articulated singly. In playing rapid notes, the problem is getting them to speak, not playing them short or staccato. So the student is advised to concentrate on maintaining air pressure, using a soft, relaxed tongue, and continually increasing speed in his articulation studies.

The problem of synchronization that often occurs in both single and multiple tonguing is aided most by accenting the groups of notes in twos, threes, or fours, to keep tongue, fingers, and mind together. When evenness and accuracy are achieved, the accent must be retained mentally but not be apparent to the listener.

Another basic principle of tonguing used in several multiple articulations is the rolled *r*, common to the Latin languages. When used in music literature, it is termed flutter-tongue (G. *Flatterzunge*; F. *Rrrr*), or notated as follows:

This articulation is based on a rapid flutter of the tip of the tongue, with the tongue shaped as in the syllable *tr* or *dr*. Both of these are possible and should be tried, with the tongue curved up at the sides to close off the mouth chamber, and air forced past the tongue at sufficient pressure to vibrate it.

Some experimentation may be necessary to determine the correct relationship between tongue tension and air pressure. In beginning attempts at this type of articulation, the student will normally find it easier to start in the middle or even the upper register. The greater resistance of this range makes the flutter tongue easier to produce. The lowest octave is the most difficult in which to use the flutter tongue successfully, but a very open throat will help. A guttural throat vibration, *grrr,* may sometimes be used as a substitute, and often is used in the low range even by flutists who can successfully use the normal flutter tongue in the rest of the range.

The single flutter of the Latin *r* is identical to the English *d* articulation, and is used in several types of flute articulation. Its use in double and triple tonguing has already been discussed in Chapter IV. Its application to dotted-note rhythms also deserves study.

Moderate-to-fast rhythms, such as the following, will be articulated easier and more accurately if the long notes are tongued with a *d* syllable, as indicated:

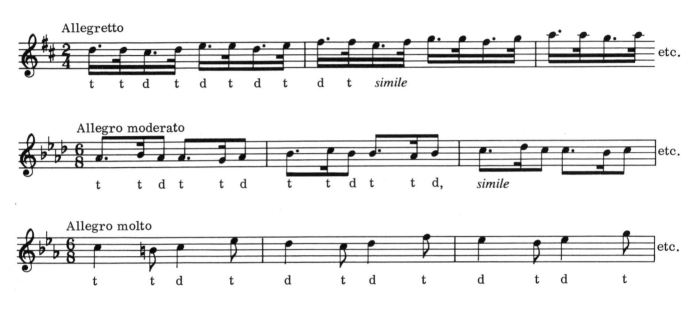

In very fast tempos a modified double tongue becomes preferable, with the *k* syllable on the short note.

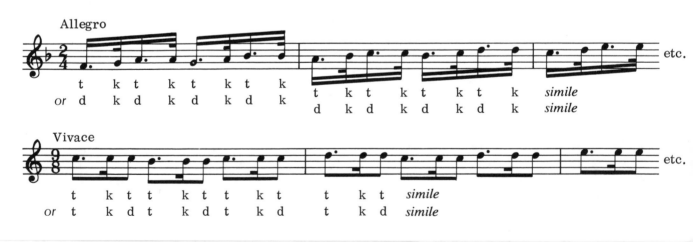

CHAPTER IX

TECHNICAL DEVELOPMENT

FINGER DEXTERITY

The development of finger technique depends on both physical and mental attributes, but concentration on the physical aspects also aids the development of mental speed and accuracy. Of prime importance is the insistence on correct hand and finger position, and the use of only the basic fingerings to develop the necessary facility and independence of the fingers.

Finger exercises must be practiced with a light, relaxed technique, in a soft or moderate dynamic range, speeded up gradually, and slowed down again when the hands become tense.

The ideal to strive for in finger action is the minimum motion and effort needed to close or open the keys. This is very light muscle action through a distance of about an eighth of an inch. Greater finger effort is wasted, and wider movement interferes with both speed and evenness of technique.

The insistence on basic fingering is important not only to develop the fingers, but to aid in sight-reading, where there is no time to figure out alternate fingerings for difficult passages.

The exercises that follow are the most rapid approach to independence of the ring fingers of each hand, if the right little finger is depressed when called for. The flutist should be aware that independence of these fingers is probably the most important physical aspect of finger technique.

For the right hand:

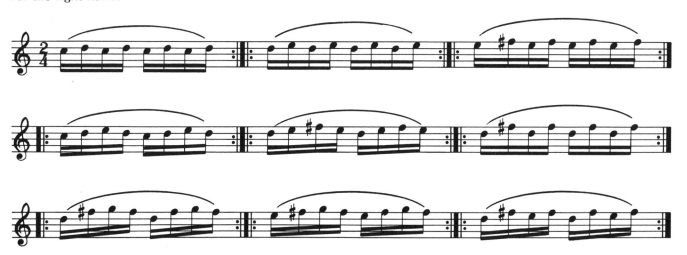

For the left hand:

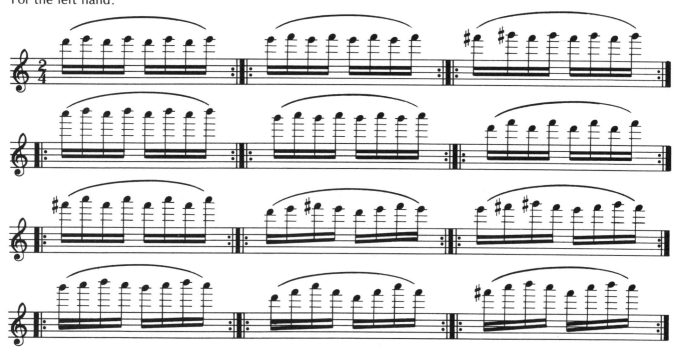

In addition, the student should be thoroughly familiar with the following types of studies, preferably without reading the notes:

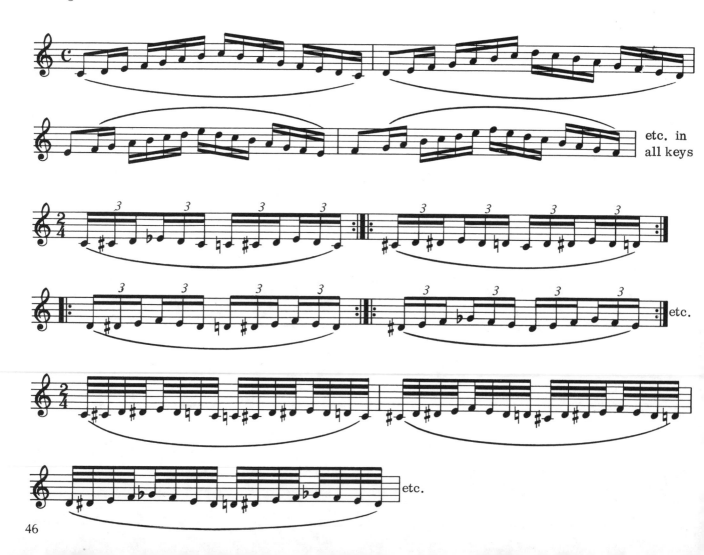

etc. in all keys

etc.

etc.

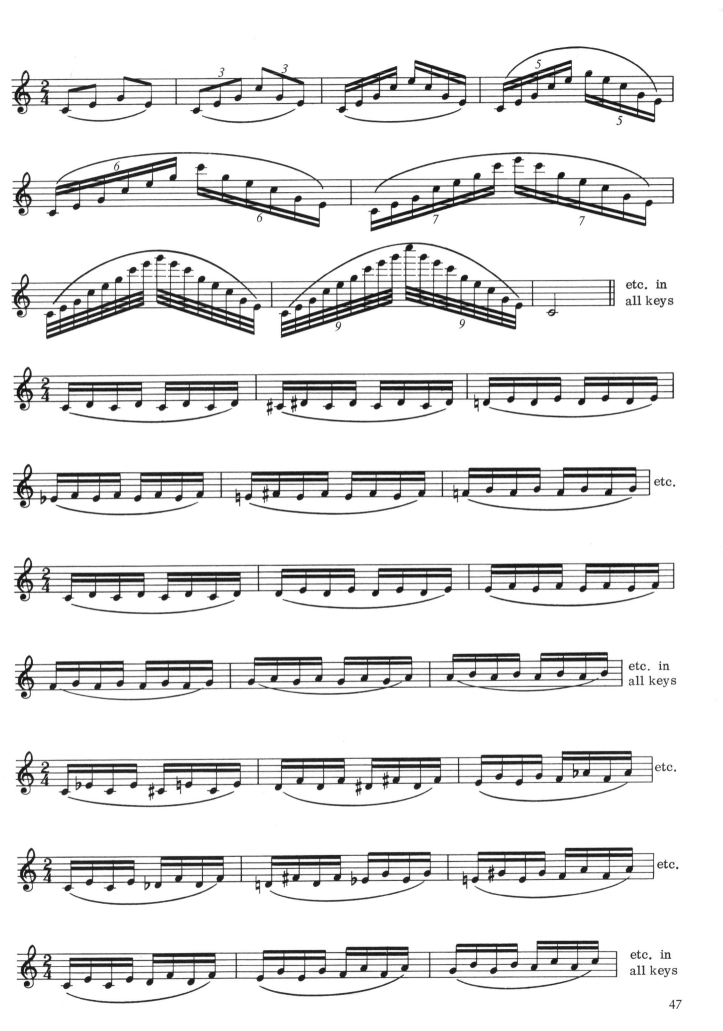

etc. in all keys

etc.

etc. in all keys

etc.

etc.

etc. in all keys

47

All of these studies should be slurred in practice to expose any unevenness in fingering. They are also excellent tonguing studies, and should be practiced in varied articulations as the student becomes more advanced. Slow practice at the start of each study is recommended, to point out possible unevenness.

The student must also become conscious of the difference in lifting and depressing pads in reference to response. In lifting a pad, the pitch changes almost immediately, but in depressing a pad the tone doesn't change until after the key has moved about an eighth of an inch. Slow study will soon reveal this distinction.

To develop maximum facility with the right little finger, the following studies should also be mastered:

In descending from E, F, F♯, etc., to low C or C♯, the right little finger should be lifted before it is needed, but in ascending, the finger should slide between keys.

TRILLS AND TREMOLOS

The student should memorize the following trill and tremolo charts so that he can cover the range of the flute chromatically in intervals of half steps, whole steps, minor thirds, etc., without reference to the charts. These should also be learned both with and without the terminal turn, as illustrated:

Trills should also be practiced for speed, while remembering that a nervous shake is seldom an effective trill. The motion of the finger or fingers involved must be a definite action. This allows the notes to speak, and avoids having the trill stop because the fingers freeze from excessive tension.

In all trills involving the use of the auxiliary trill keys in the right hand, the flutist should develop the habit of shifting his fingers to the left: the upper trill key is operated by the second finger, and the lower trill key is operated by the ring finger. This is to avoid the problem of some combinations of fingerings in which the fingers are taken out of position for the notes that follow.

The only exception to this position is in the combination of high F♯ and B, where sliding the finger between keys should be avoided.

*R. H. 2nd finger on trill key   ** T1 3 / 2 E♭

In addition, the student should develop the habit of operating these trill keys with the fingers well back at the base of the keys, to avoid simultaneously depressing a neighboring key.

Key to Fingering Charts

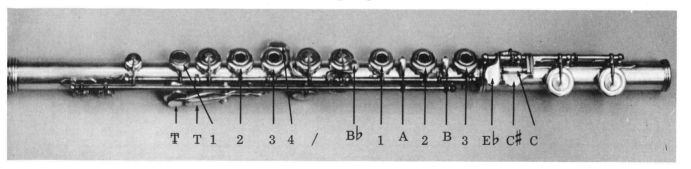

✗ = Half-hole, on French model flutes.

① = Key or keys to be activated.

The most common fingering is given first in each case. All trill, tremolando, and alternate fingerings should be compared with regular fingerings for quality and intonation, since there is considerable variation between flutes.

Close C# key with right knee, middle joint of little finger, toothpick, or rubber band and trill with C key.

 T123 /123 Ⓒ#

 T123 /123Ⓔ♭

 T123 /12③ E♭

 T123 /1② E♭

 T123 /① 3E♭

 T123 / ③E♭
T123 /② E♭
(when followed by turn on E)

 T123④/ E♭

 T12㉞/ E♭
T12③4/ E♭

 T̶1② / E♭
T1② / ᴮ♭ E♭
T1② /1 E♭

 T1 /① E♭
T1 / Ⓑ♭ E♭

 Ⓣ1 / E♭

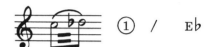 ① / E♭

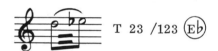 /Ⓐ E♭

 T 23 /123 Ⓔ♭

 same as lower octave

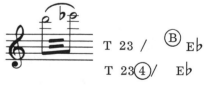 T 23 / Ⓑ E♭
T 23④/ E♭

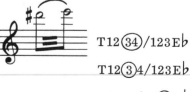 T12㉞/123E♭
T12③4/123E♭
T1234/12③E♭

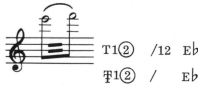 T1② /12 E♭
T̶1② / E♭

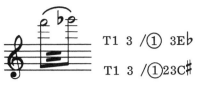

T1 3 /① 3Eb
T1 3 /①23C#

Ⓣ1 3 / 3Eb
Ⓣ1 3 / 2 Eb
(when followed by turn on E)
123 /① C#

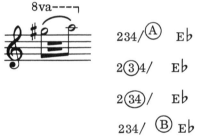

123 / Ⓐ Eb

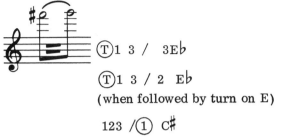

234/Ⓐ Eb
2③4/ Eb
2(34)/ Eb
234/ Ⓑ Eb

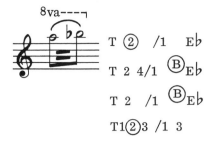

T ② /1 Eb
T 2 4/1 ⒷEb
T 2 /1 ⒷEb
T1②3 /1 3

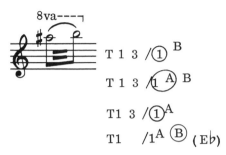

T 1 3 /① B
T 1 3 /1 Ⓐ B
T1 3 /①A
T1 /1A Ⓑ (Eb)

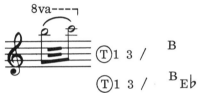

Ⓣ1 3 / B
Ⓣ1 3 / B Eb

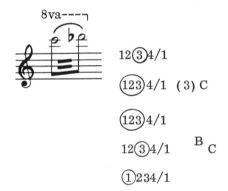

12③4/1
(123)4/1 (3) C
(123)4/1
12③4/1 B C
①234/1

 T123 /123 Ⓒ

 T123 /123C♯

Hook thumbnail behind D key on
open–hole flute, or close C♯ key
with rubber band or toothpick
and trill E♭ key.

 T123 /12 ③

 T123 /1 ㉓ E♭

T123 /1 ② 3E♭

 T123 /① 2 E♭

 T123 /① E♭

 T123 ④/ 3E♭

T123 ④/ 2 E♭
(when followed by turn on E)

 T12 ③ / E♭

 T1② 34/ E♭

T1② 34/ ᴮ♭ E♭

T1② 34/1 E♭

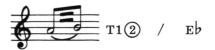 T1② / E♭

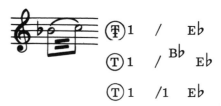 Ⓣ1 / E♭

Ⓣ1 / ᴮ♭ E♭

Ⓣ1 /1 E♭

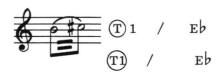 Ⓣ1 / E♭

Ⓣ1 / E♭

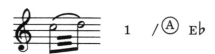 1 /Ⓐ E♭

 /Ⓑ E♭

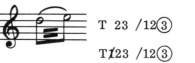 T 23 /12③

T♯23 /12③
(L.H. first finger is half-closed)

 } same as lower octave

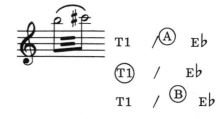 T1 /Ⓐ E♭

Ⓣ1 / E♭

T1 / Ⓑ E♭

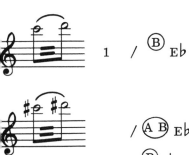

1 / Ⓑ Eb

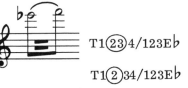

/ ⒶⒷ Eb

/ Ⓑ Eb

2⌿ / ⒶⒷ Eb

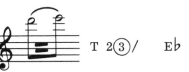

T 2③/ Eb

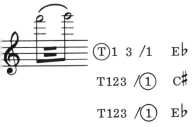

T1㉓4/123 Eb

T1②34/123 Eb

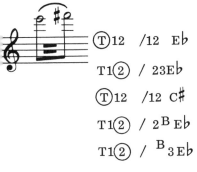

Ⓣ12 /12 Eb

T1② / 23 Eb

Ⓣ12 /12 C#

T1② / 2ᴮ Eb

T1② / ᴮ3 Eb

Ⓣ1 3 /1 Eb

T123 /① C#

T123 /① Eb

Ⓣ1 **3** / 3 Eb

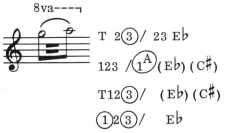

T 2③/ 23 Eb

123 /1ᴬ (Eb)(C#)

T12③/ (Eb)(C#)

①2③/ Eb

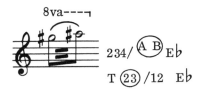

234/ ⒶⒷ Eb

T㉓/12 Eb

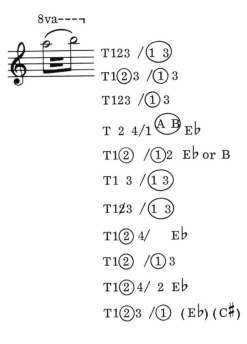

T123 /① 3

T1②3 /① 3

T123 /① 3

T 2 4/1 ⒶⒷ Eb

T1② /①2 Eb or B

T1 3 /① 3

T1⌿3 /① 3

T1② 4/ Eb

T1② /① 3

T1②4/ 2 Eb

T1②3 /① (Eb)(C#)

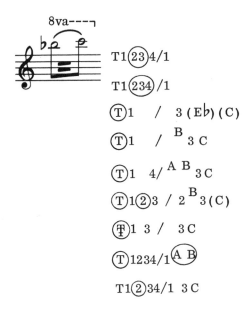

T1㉓4/1

T1㈢/1

Ⓣ1 / 3 (Eb)(C)

Ⓣ1 / ᴮ3 C

Ⓣ1 4/ ᴬᴮ3 C

Ⓣ1②3 / 2ᴮ3(C)

Ⓣ1 3 / 3 C

Ⓣ1234/1 ⒶⒷ

T1②34/1 3 C

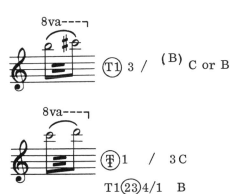

Ⓣ1 3 / (B) C or B

Ⓣ1 / 3 C

T1㉓4/1 B

Minor Third Tremolandos

 Close C key with right knee, rubber band, or toothpick and trill E♭ key.

 T123 /12③C♯
T123 /12⟨3C♯⟩

 T123 /1⟨23⟩

 T123 /⟨12⟩3 E♭

 T123 /⟨12⟩ E♭

 T123④/1 E♭

 T12③/ 3 E♭

 T̶1⟨23⟩/ E♭
T1⟨23⟩/ᴮ♭ E♭

 T1⟨23⟩4/ E♭
T1⟨2⟩34/ E♭

 ⟨T⟩1⟨2⟩ / E♭
⟨T⟩12 /123 E♭
⟨T⟩12 / E♭

 ⟨T̶1⟩ / E♭
⟨T1⟩ /ᴮ♭ E♭
⟨T1⟩ /1 E♭
T̶1 𝄽 /⟨A⟩ E♭
(in piano)

 T1 /⟨A⟩ E♭
T1 /⟨1⟩⟨B⟩E♭

 1 /⟨A B⟩ E♭

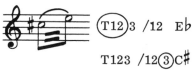 ⟨T12⟩3 /12 E♭
T123 /12③C♯
⟨T1⟩23 /12 E♭

 T123 /1⟨23⟩

 T123 /⟨12⟩3 E♭

 } same as lower octave

54

⊤1̃ / E♭

T1 /B♭ E♭

T1 /1 E♭

T123 /1̃2̃3E♭

T123 /1̃23E♭

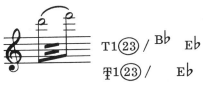

T123 /1̃2̃ E♭

T1 3 /Ã B̃ E♭

T1 /Ã B̃ E♭

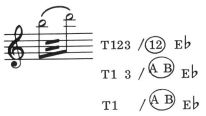

1 /Ã B̃ E♭

T12③ / 3 E♭

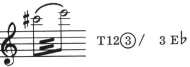

T1②③ /B♭ E♭

⊤1②③ / E♭

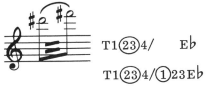

T1②③4/ E♭

T1②③4/1̃23E♭

⊤1② / E♭

8va---¬

⊤1̃ / E♭

8va---¬

T1②̸34/1̃Ã C♯

T12③/ ③C♯

8va---¬

⊤1②③ / E♭

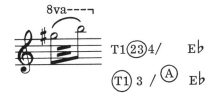

8va---¬

T1②③4/ E♭

⊤1̃ 3 /Ã E♭

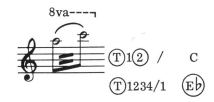

8va---¬

⊤1② / C

⊤1234/1 E♭

Major Third Tremolandos

 T123 /12③C

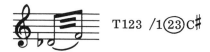 T123 /1②③C#

 T123 /⑫3

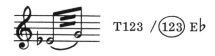 T123 /①②③ Eb

 T123④/1　Eb

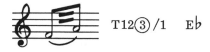 T12③/1　Eb

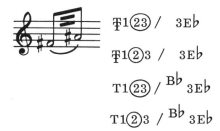
T̶1②③/　3Eb
T̶1②3/　3Eb
T1②③/ Bb 3Eb
T1②3/ Bb 3Eb

 T1②③/　Eb

Ⓣ1②34/　Eb
T①234/　Eb
Ⓣ1234/　Eb

Ⓣ12 /　Eb
T12 /Ⓐ Eb

T̶1 3 /① Ⓑ Eb
T̶1 /Ⓑ Eb

 T1 /Ⓐ Ⓑ Eb

T123 /12③ C
Ⓣ1②3 /12 Eb

T123 /1②③C#
Ⓣ12 3 /1　Eb

 } same as lower octave

T123 /①②③ Eb
T̶1 /Ⓐ Ⓑ Eb

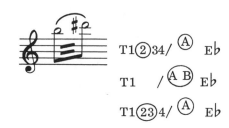
T1②34/ Ⓐ Eb
T1 /Ⓐ Ⓑ Eb
T1②③4/ Ⓐ Eb

 T12③/① Eb

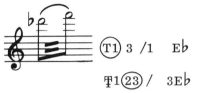 T̶1 3 /1 Eb

T̶1②③/ 3Eb

 T1②③/ Eb

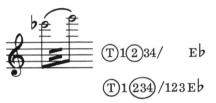 Ⓣ1②34/ Eb

Ⓣ1②③④/123 Eb

 T12 / Eb

 T̶1②̶3̶ /1ᴬ C#

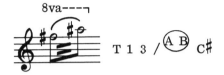 T 1 3 /Ⓐ Ⓑ C#

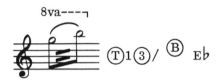 Ⓣ1③/ Ⓑ Eb

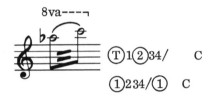 Ⓣ1②34/ C

①234/① C

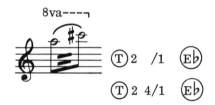 Ⓣ2 /1 Ⓔ♭

Ⓣ2 4/1 Ⓔ♭

Perfect Fourth Tremolandos

 T123 /1(23) C

 T123 /(12)3C♯

 T123 /(123)

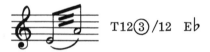 T123(4)/(1)23E♭
alternate

 T12(3)/12 E♭

 T1(23)/1 E♭

 T1(2)3 / 3E♭

(T)1(2)3 / E♭

 T(12)34/ E♭
T1234/ (B) E♭

 T12 / (B) E♭

 T̄1 / (A B) E♭

 T1(23)/(12 B) E♭

 same as lower octave

 (T12) /(A) E♭
alternate

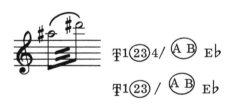 T̄1(23)4/ (A B) E♭
T̄1(23) / (A B) E♭

 T1(2) /(12 B) E♭

T123 /⑫3C

T123 /⑫③C♯

T123④/123

T123④/①23
alternate

T12③/123E♭

T1②③/12 E♭

T1②③/① E♭
(poor)

Ⓣ1②3 / 3E♭

Ⓣ123 / 3E♭

T123 /Ⓐ E♭

T⑫3 / E♭

T1234/ Ⓑ E♭

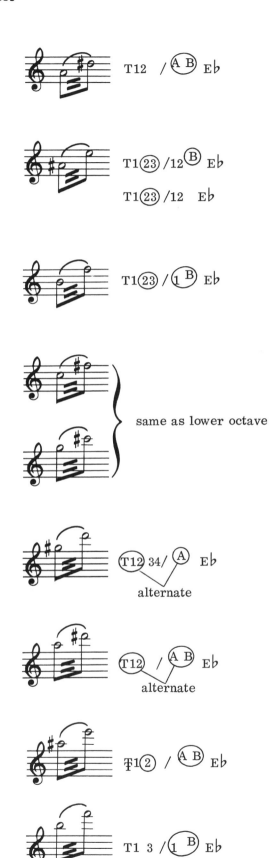

T12 /Ⓐ Ⓑ E♭

T1②③/12Ⓑ E♭

T1②③/12 E♭

T1②③/①Ⓑ E♭

same as lower octave

Ⓣ12 34/Ⓐ E♭
alternate

Ⓣ12 /Ⓐ Ⓑ E♭
alternate

T̶1② /Ⓐ Ⓑ E♭

T1 3 /①Ⓑ E♭

 T123 /⟨123⟩ C

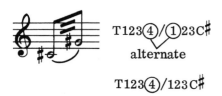 T123④/①23C♯
alternate
T123④/123C♯

 T12③/123

 T1⟨23⟩/123E♭

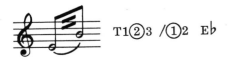 T1②3 /①2 E♭

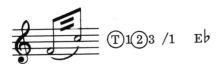 ⟨T⟩1②3 /1 E♭

 T⟨12⟩3 / 3E♭
T123 /⟨B⟩ 3E♭

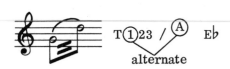 T①23 /⟨A⟩ E♭
alternate

 T1234/ ⟨A B⟩ E♭

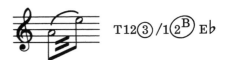 T12③/1⟨2 B⟩ E♭

 T1⟨23⟩ / ⟨B⟩ E♭

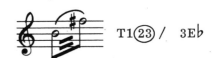 T1⟨23⟩ / 3E♭

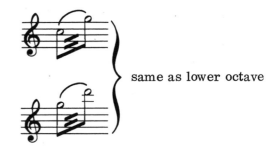 same as lower octave

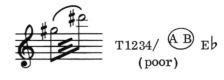 T1234/ ⟨A B⟩ E♭
(poor)

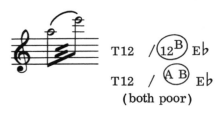 T12 /⟨12 B⟩ E♭
T12 / ⟨A B⟩ E♭
(both poor)

 T1③/1 ⟨B⟩ E♭

ALTISSIMO FINGERINGS

In each instance, the most common fingering is listed first.
The additional fingerings are for reasons of response, intonation or facility.

Altissimo Fingerings

1234/1

1234/1 3C

1234/1 B gizmo

123 /1 ^{B}3(C)

1234/123

T1234/1 3C

1234/12^B C or B

1 3 / ^{B} (E♭)

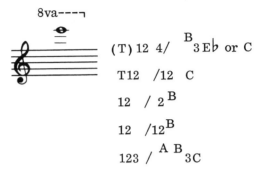

(T) 12 4/ ^{B}3 E♭ or C

T12 /12 C

12 / 2^B

12 /12^B

123 / $^{A\ B}$3C

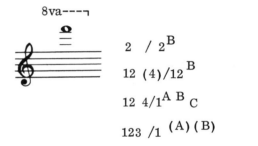

2 / 2^B

12 (4)/12 ^{B}

12 4/1$^{A\ B}$ C

123 /1 (A)(B)

2 /1 3C

2 4/1

2 /1

2 /1 C

2 4/1   C

12 /1 3 (C)

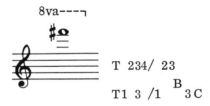

T 234/ 23

T1 3 /1 ^{B}3C

8va---

T 3 /12 C

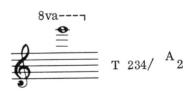

8va---

T 234/ ^{A}2

8va---

T 34/ ^{A}2 C

T1234/1 $^{(A)}$3(E♭)

T 3 /1 $^{(A)}$ E♭ or C

T 3 / ^{A}2 C

ALTERNATE FINGERINGS

The fingerings in the following charts are used to facilitate difficult fingerings, to ensure security of response, or to alter pitch on tones that are relatively hard to control. Generally, these fingerings are not used unless absolutely necessary. The basic fingerings must be firmly established habits before these alternates are introduced.

In addition to these alternate fingerings, trill fingerings are always available to facilitate passages, as are the harmonics at the twelfth and at two octaves. In most instances, a troublesome group of notes will need only one or possibly two alternate fingerings to make it easier. An entire group of notes will very seldom warrant special fingering, and because these fingerings are always of relatively poor quality and pitch, they must only be used as a last resort, not as a panacea for lazy technique.

In problematic groups of notes it is best to use the regular fingering on the most prominent notes: the first and last notes of the group, or any note that is accented. Trying the following examples should make this evident:

* Use trill fingering on third note of each group only

Polovtsian Dance

A. Borodin

* Use trill fingerings

Classical Symphony

S. Prokofiev

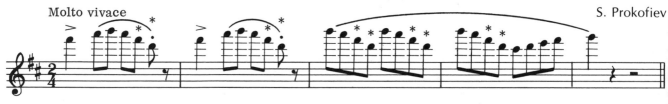

* Use harmonic at the twelfth to produce these tones.

62

Chart of Alternate Fingerings

1   /123

T12₃ /   E♭

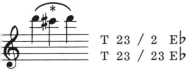

T 23 / 2 E♭
T 23 / 23 E♭

T123 /   E♭

T1 3 /123E♭

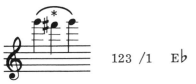

123 /1   E♭

T 234/12 E♭

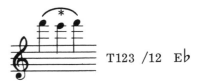

T 23 /123C♯   /123

T 23 /12 E♭

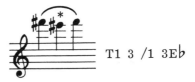

3 /123 E♭

T123 /12 E♭

T1 3 /1 3E♭

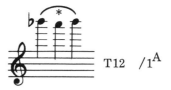

T 23 /123E♭

T12 /1ᴬ

The above lower alternates are particularly useful in turns following trills. For upper alternates, the normal trill fingerings are used.

T1 3 /1ᴬ ᴮ

In the following arpeggiated examples, the right ring finger may be kept depressed throughout, except for the final tone.

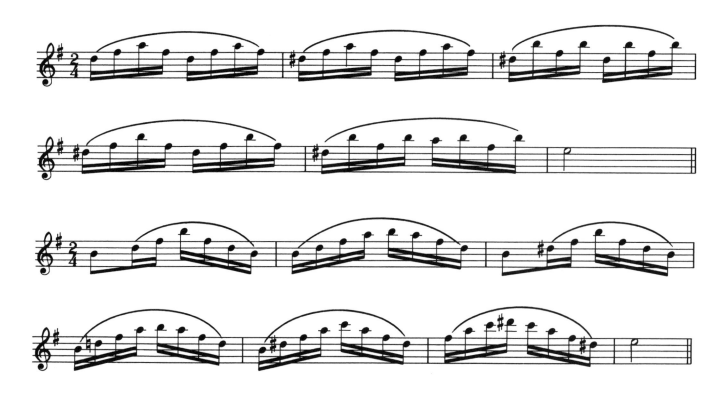

Examples including the following patterns may be played with the right little finger up and the first, second, and third fingers depressed throughout.

The execution of chords such as E♭ minor or F♯ major may be facilitated by using the thumb B♭ if the right little finger is not depressed.

The B♭ lever activated by the right forefinger is particularly useful in trill patterns such as the following, and in chromatic scales.

/123
to alternate with D

/123Eb
to alternate with D#

123 /123C#
lowers pitch

T 23 /1 A♮23
raises pitch

T 23 /1 A♮23Eb

T 23 /123Eb
both raise pitch

T123 /12 Eb
T123 /12 B Eb
both raise pitch

T123 /1 3Eb

T123 /12 Eb

123 /1 Eb
all raise pitch

T 23 / Eb

T12 /12
secure in forte and
in approach from above

T12 /12 B Eb
secure in approach from below

T1 3 /1 C#
more secure and raises pitch

T1 3 / 3C#
more secure and raises pitch

T1 3 / 2 Eb
lowers pitch

234/ 23Eb

234/ 23Eb
more secure and lowers pitch

T 2 4/1 Eb
more secure

T 2 /1 3C#
raises pitch

8va----¬

T1 3 / A 3
raises pitch

8va----¬

T1 3 / A B 3Eb

T1 3 / A B 3C

T1 3 / A B 3Eb

T1 3 / 3

T1 3 / A B B gizmo
all of the above lower pitch

8va----¬

1234/12
123 /12
both lower pitch

1234/1 3C
123 /1 3C
both raise pitch

 T1234/ (C♯ A) E♭

 T1 / (C♯ B) E♭

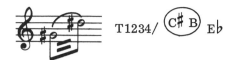 T1234/ (C♯ B) E♭

 1 / (C♯ B) E♭

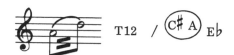 T12 / (C♯ A) E♭

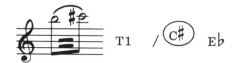 T1 / (C♯) E♭

 T12 / (C♯ B) E♭

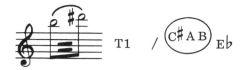 T1 / (C♯ A B) E♭

 T1 / (C♯ A) E♭

 1 / (C♯ A B) E♭

 T1 / (C♯ B) E♭

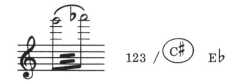 123 / (C♯) E♭

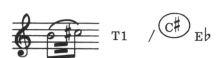 T1 / (C♯) E♭

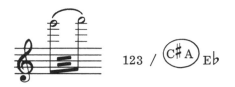 123 / (C♯ A) E♭

 T1 / (C♯ A) E♭

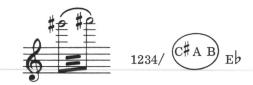 1234/ (C♯ A B) E♭

CHAPTER X

POINTERS ON PERFORMANCE

RHYTHM AND ARTICULATION

The importance of the physical aspects of rhythm should be continually emphasized. The student must be conscious of the importance of feeling a secure pulse as a framework within which tones are apportioned time. To this end, the beginner should be encouraged to tap his foot, bounce up and down, or do whatever proves necessary to establish a feeling of rhythmic pulse.

In performance these movements are not desirable but can easily be curbed, whereas the lack of a rhythmic pulse in performance is intolerable.

After a secure feeling of rhythmic pulse is achieved the student may experiment with rubato interpretations. Rubato cannot be successful unless the performer has a strong sense of rhythm that persists throughout the variations of a rubato passage.

Although rubato is usually confined to the space between bar lines, it may at times extend longer. A valuable study is the practice of rubato playing with a metronome, so that each downbeat coincides with the basic pulse.

This strong feeling of basic pulse is also one of the most valuable assets in sight-reading, in that it maintains a rhythmic framework for the performer even though some small errors in playing may occur.

When a phrase begins with an opening rest or has a rest on a major accent, the performer must feel this missing beat so he can perform the phrase accurately. Breathing on the empty beat, as well as tapping the foot or toe, should be sufficient.

This sense of rhythm is also essential in playing the many varieties of syncopation. The student must feel the missing accent to play the pattern correctly. When a syncopated figure proves difficult to master, the introduction of this accent will help to learn the pattern, but it should be omitted in performance.

Sonata in B Minor

J. S. Bach

Some articulation patterns can also be factors in disturbing rhythm because they are difficult to play evenly. In the first instance below, the tendency is to play the first note too short or fast in relation to the other three. This is corrected by placing a slight accent, or even tenuto stress, on the first note.

In the other two examples, the tendency is to be late with the second note of the group, and it should be anticipated to assure evenness. In each instance it may be necessary to study the figure quite slowly at first to establish an even pattern, and then gradually speed up.

These patterns should also be practiced at rapid tempos with the following multiple articulations:

In the example below, the student should realize that the first articulation is usually recommended and very effective at moderate speeds, but the second will be more practical at rapid tempos:

Staccato notes should get heavier and longer, as well as louder, when playing longer phrases in crescendo. Only in this way can sufficient sound be produced on each note.

In marcato playing the performer must shorten the notes as well as accent them.

When called on to play three notes in the time of two, or two in the time of three, the smallest common multiple, six, is used to ensure accuracy. Two notes in three beats, for example, is relatively easy, since the second tone starts in the middle of the second subdivision.

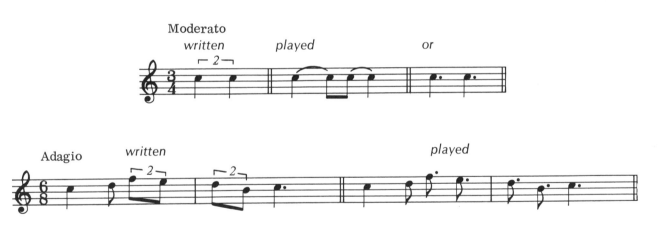

Three notes in two beats is slightly more difficult since the performer must think in triplets on the two beats or subdivisions, and place the notes as illustrated:

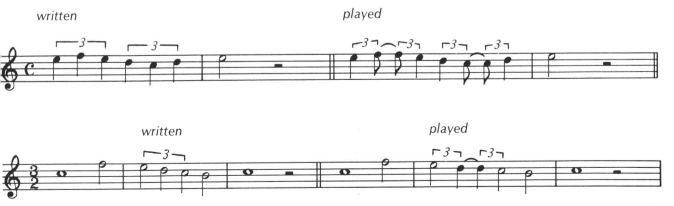

Whenever groups of both two and three are found near each other in a passage, great care must be exerted to avoid distorting one or the other. The predominant figure should be subdivided as on page 69, so that the less common group may be played accurately.

Sonata (1936)

To play four notes in three beats, the least common multiple of twelve is used, as follows:

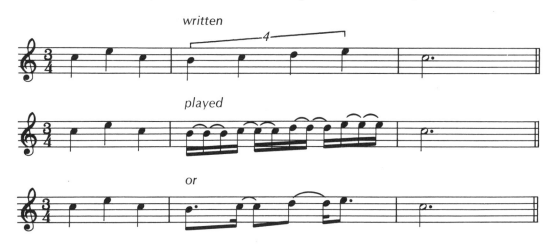

Slow practice is necessary to establish a feeling for this subdivision. Then it can be speeded up without the mechanics of counting twelves.

In mastering groups of five, seven, nine, or more notes, subdividing them into smaller groups will be most helpful. The choice in subdividing will usually be based on stressing the more important notes in a group melodically or harmonically. They must still be played rhythmically equal, however; the subdivisions are intended only as mental groupings.

Night Soliloquy

K. Kennan

In articulating repeated pitches in a phrase, note that the flute tone tends to ring and run together in a hall. So it is necessary either to space the notes slightly or to stress the attack on the second note somewhat to make the articulation apparent to the listener.

Poem

C. Griffes

The "growl" as used in some jazz performances is not truly a type of articulation, but deserves mention here as worthy of development for those interested in this field. It is accomplished by humming in unison or in octaves with the notes being played, and it produces a rather rough, unusual sound.

The average male voice has an extremely limited range in terms of humming in unison, but the octave proves very effective. Female jazz flutists are a rarity, but it would be interesting to hear some of the possibilities of the unison growl by a female performer.

PHRASING AND INTERPRETATION

Some additional problems in phrasing musically merit special consideration, although the basic principles of good phrasing have already been discussed. One of the most difficult problems occurs in the long passages of rapid notes that don't allow space for breath. Often, the only solution is to omit a note for this purpose, rather than to break the rhythm. The note omitted should be near the natural phrase ending and should be least important. This will often be the last note in a measure when it is an unaccented note at the end of a sequence. But do not omit part of a pickup group of notes.

Sonata, Op. 94

S. Prokofiev

*( ) May be omitted to facilitate breathing.

Some exceptions may be tolerated when a passage is sufficiently rubato to allow a breath.

There are also times when breaths should be taken, even though not needed by the performer, to show th[e] phrase more clearly.

Sonata in F

G. F. Handel

Breathing after tied notes can be a problem in **moderate** to fast tempos. The performer will want to **feel the tie,** but then can't breathe in time. As the tempo or note speed increases, the breath must be taken b[y] actually omitting the tied note and breathing on th[e] accent.

When a phrase ends with a rest, particularly in shorter phrases or in phrases interrupted by rests, let the tone ring by not cutting it off with the tongue. This helps avoid chopping up the musical idea, but be careful to avoid letting the tone run into the rest. The best way to avoid this is by actually breathing *on* the rest. The preceding tone should be of full value, but not allowed to enter the empty beat.

Sonata in C Minor

G. P. Telemann

When dynamic indications are not detailed by the composer, the performer will do well to follow the contour of the melodic line. There is a tendency to crescendo when ascending and to relax dynamically when descending. This natural tendency should generally be followed, but with discretion.

Concerto in D

W. A. Mozart

The notation of accidentals poses problems because there are some inconsistencies in the conventions of notation. In most instances, the accidental preceding a tied note that covers several measures is intended to affect all notes under the tie.

A more troublesome use of accidentals is the inconsistency found in alterations at different octaves within a measure. An accidental used before a pitch in one octave is not supposed to affect the other octaves within that measure, but many composers have not followed this practice. The best guide is the style of composition.

Until the expansion of tonal concepts in the late nineteenth century, an accidental used in one octave could be assumed to be intended for the other octaves as well—they would generally be the same scale or arpeggio. The instances in which this is not true are usually revealed by a study of the harmonic character of the passage in question.

In music of the last century, composers have been much more accurate, and generally an accidental introduced in one octave is *not* intended to apply to other octaves.

To add interest to performances, particularly of baroque music, here are some additional points to consider. Repeated phrases or sections should be varied, if only dynamically. This should not become a cliché, however, as in the common approach to baroque music in which each section is played forte and repeated piano. In slow movements the tones may be, and in the eighteenth century commonly were, ornamented.

In repeating a section, be sure the first ending doesn't sound so final that the repeat becomes unnecessary. This is a common problem in performances of baroque music, where the temptation is to retard at every obvious cadence. New musical ideas should be emphasized, if only by dynamic change, to attach importance to the idea. The vocal quality of the flute in melodic phrases should be exploited. Don't let the phrases become run on sentences.

It is now customary for a soloist to play the tutti of the last few bars of a classic concerto (and the practice is recommended) to avoid the awkwardness of the soloist standing idle while the orchestra tacks on the codetta.

The performance of cadenzas also deserves a few special notes. Because the cadenza is an improvisational interlude, it must sound relatively extemporaneous. This means it must be very rubato and truly show off the technique of the performer.

The student must be careful not to let accelerandos get out of control, but he must make the most of what he is able to manage. Usually, this will mean starting passages that demand accelerando well below tempo, so that there is room for the acceleration.

Generally, all aspects of interpretation should be exaggerated; a crescendo must be a big one, pianissimo can be a whisper, extra time should be taken with fermati and obvious phrases. Passagework in scales, arpeggios, etc., must be rhythmically free enough to avoid sounding like an exercise, but the basic tempo of the cadenza is still derived from the movement in which it appears.

Since the glissando is appearing more and more frequently in contemporary music, it should also be thoroughly understood. Notated in several ways, it is accomplished by a chromatic scale, or a portion of one.

When the interval is not too great, an entire chromatic segment may be interpolated between the notes. On smaller intervals, the open-hole flute allows an even more effective glissando by making it possible to slide onto or off the keys in passing. Longer glissandos, or those involving longer note values, are often reduced to only portions of the chromatics included, with the middle of the glissando omitted.

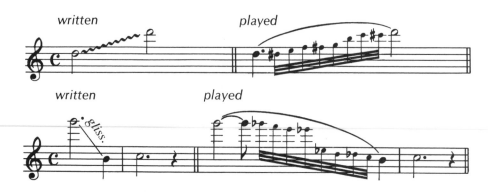

In modern arrangements of popular music, two additional techniques have become common, the *bend* and the *smear*. These may vary from a half step, using the open hole if possible, to three or more chromatic tones.

Bend

ritten   played

Smear

ritten   played

Note that in hearing a vibrato, the ear interprets the
per level as the true pitch, rather than a mean of the
tch amplitude.

To realize the possibilities of the flute further, advise
e student to study the performances of artists on other
struments. Violinists can expand his concepts of
ticulation. Most bow techniques can be remarkably
ll imitated by the tongue. Pianists provide excellent
amples of the use of rubato for interest and
pressiveness. Vocalists also deserve study for rubato
d expressive techniques, as well as for valuable lessons
phrasing and breathing.

E OF VIBRATO

Control of both speed and amplitude of vibrato is most
sirable in flute playing because of the extensive variety
musical requirements. The basic techniques of
idying vibrato are treated on page 17. Its use in
rformance deserves more detailed consideration.

The pulsations of vibrato affect several of the basic
aracteristics of tone: pitch, intensity, and timbre. The
eal flute vibrato is accomplished by varying the
tensity of sound, although pitch and timbre are also

slightly affected. Since blowing harder causes the pitch
to rise, and the converse is also true, using an intensity
vibrato will slightly change the pitch unless
compensating adjustments are made.

Amplitude of
pitch vibrato

pitch heard
here ~~~~~~ not here ~~~~~~

For this reason, care must be exercised that the pitch
does not rise when adding vibrato to a tone.

Vibrato also causes changes in the harmonic structure
of tones, tending to all strength to the upper partials and
thus adding to the brilliance of tone. This factor is most
useful in adding life to a tone after it is introduced. or in
allowing a tone to become duller in morendo by slowing
and finally stopping the vibrato as the tone diminishes.

Be sure to emphasize, though, that vibrato is
essentially an ornament to the tone. It cannot
compensate for poor tonal quality, nor can it make up
for faulty intonation!

Because of differences in resistance in the several
registers of the flute, a wider amplitude in vibrato is
desirable in the upper range, whereas a narrower
vibrato is best in the low octave. The upper range
usually also requires a faster vibrato, while a relatively
slower vibrato will be more satisfactory in the lower
range.

Dynamics must also be considered, since louder
dynamics will generally demand a faster vibrato, while
softer dynamics call for a slower speed. This is especially
obvious in crescendo and diminuendo, as a minimum of
experiment will demonstrate.

Vibrato is seldom used in passages consisting of many
rapid notes because it interferes with response and
clarity. It may, however, be used to point up tenuto or
prominent tones in this same type of passage.

The Song of the Wind

J. Donjon

Vibrato should be used only to emphasize the tones marked tenuto.

INTONATION IN ENSEMBLE

Remember that the flute is probably the most accurate wind instrument in regard to intonation, and the performer is responsible for the minute variations necessary in performance. With the flute head-joint pulled out about an eighth of an inch, the instrument is designed to produce a concert pitch of A = 440 vibrations per second. Some flutes are manufactured (usually upon request) with a higher pitch level, and the purchaser of a used instrument should be aware of this.

In initial tuning with an ensemble, the flutist must set his instrument as above, to establish a starting point for his pitch. An A or Bb for tuning purposes should be a full sound with a firm attack, and must not be humored. The purpose is to determine one's relationship to the pitch as given by the oboe or piano, not to see if one can play in tune with it.

Rolling the flute in or out while tuning is only to determine if one's basic pitch is above or below the given standard. When the pitches are very close, the beats between the two also help to find the proper adjustment in the head-joint setting that must be made.

In humoring tones in performance, reliance must be on the lip and jaw, as discussed on page 11, not on rolling the flute in or out, or bobbing the head up and down. These latter techniques are resorted to only in extreme situations, such as the necessity to keep the pitch up at the end of a morendo.

Accurate intonation is a constant procedure of humoring tones in relation to their harmonic and melodic peculiarities, as well as in relation to the other instruments in ensemble.

Compromises of mechanism make it necessary to design the flute on the principles of tempered tuning. But we hear and play in a combination of just and Pythagorean intonation. Thus, perfect intervals (octaves, fifths, etc.) will want to be heard in true relationship, while major intervals will require expansion, and minor intervals will need to be made smaller.

Tendency tones, such as the leading tone of a key, or the seventh of minor and diminished structures, will want to be humored in the direction of their tendency to resolve.

Note also that the ear tends to hear octaves stretched— that is, with the upper tone slightly higher than in a true relationship. Playing an instrument in the upper range of the orchestra, the flutist must be very acutely aware of this problem and train himself to hear true octaves. Many flutists find it helpful to adjust the head cork about one thirty-second of an inch out from the standard setting to allow for easier control. This tends to make the upper register slightly lower in pitch, and the low octave somewhat higher. Since these ranges can easily be humored in the opposite direction, this adjustment of the head cork is a valuable aid if done with discretion.

The flutist should also be aware that instrumentalists are usually more comfortable when playing slightly above their neighbor's pitch. One must train himself to hear the center of his tone as low as possible in matching pitches.

The obvious discomfort of actually playing flat will usually preclude the possibility of going too far in this direction, but the tendency to play slightly sharp has no limits. When two instrumentalists sound a pitch slightly above and below each other, the low pitch is the one that sounds out of tune!

The basic intonation of the flute is excellent, but we should also understand its pitch peculiarities. Because of the compromises necessary in determining the size and position of each hole, some tones may be humored in one direction easier than in the other. Tones that are difficult to raise in pitch include:

Notes that are difficult to lower in pitch include:

Take particular care to avoid overblowing the following notes because, although they are essentially in good relationship, they may be blown extremely sharp:

Constant attention to pitch and intonation should enable the flutist in time to hear all pitches truly before he plays them. This skill should include being able to imagine the exact pitch of his instrument to the extent that he can join other instruments already playing and match their pitch upon entrance. This depends on aural memory of pitch and memory of the physical placement of embouchure and jaw—certainly a worthy goal toward which to work.

ORNAMENTATION

Because of the extensive amount of ornamentation in flute literature, including the baroque, some additional comments on this aspect of performance warrant clarification.

Trills should generally start on the principal note and
[alte]rnate with the next note above, *in the key,* unless a
[chr]omatic alteration is indicated.

[T]he basic trill used in baroque music begins with the
[upp]er note, if it is not already preceded by that note.
[Thi]s appoggiatura must be on the beat, and should not
[be c]onfused with the grace note, which is played before
[the] beat.

In slower tempos, this appoggiatura is often stressed
in a tenuto fashion. Trills in the baroque style are
almost invariably ended with either a turn or an
anticipation, at the discretion of the performer.

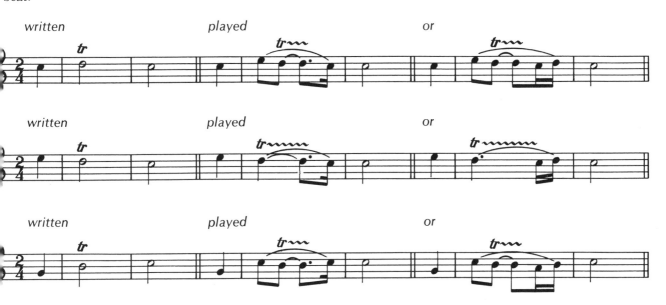

[I]n the classic style, the trill is usually terminated with
[a t]urn if it occurs at the end of a phrase or section. Trills

occurring within the phrase do not ordinarily have this
terminal turn, unless the composer has indicated it.

Concerto in D

Allegro aperto

W. A. Mozart

Sometimes the turn will sound better as a half step,
[eve]n though the key suggests a whole step. The
[pe]rformer must be the judge in this case, but the
[alt]eration will usually imply a leading tone to the
[do]minant.

Turns, when used at the end of trills, should generally
be at the speed of the trill. The novice tends to stop the
trill in preparation for the turn but must practice
keeping the trill going as long as possible to avoid this
habit. It often helps to think of the turn in relation to the
beat that follows, rather than the beat of which it is a
part.

Trills, grace notes, turns, mordents, etc., usually take
their character from the character of the music in which
they appear. In faster tempos, they are fast, and depend
upon the alternate trill fingerings. In slower tempos,
they are more relaxed, and may even use regular

written   played

fingerings for the better intonation and quality they afford.

Longer trills, whether the result of tempo or note value, will be more effective if they begin quite deliberately and with the regular fingering for the first few notes.

To play true grace notes accurately, the flutist shou understand that they tend to add a type of accent to t note to which they are attached. In performance, th note should be somewhat accented accordingly. Th will also avoid the tendency to fall onto the second no too soon after the grace note.

Trills in the upper octave of the flute, which often depend on remote harmonics, are better in quality if a closed throat is used (as in the vowel *e*), to discourage the lower partials from sounding through the trill.

Some problems in interpretation also occur because the notation of trills. The figure below can be played several ways.

In slower tempos, the value of the final note may be retained. But in moderate tempos, or note values, Example *B* will most often be preferable because it retains the dotted intent. In faster tempos or note values,

Example *C* or *D* will prove more practical.

In baroque music, particularly in slower tempos, tl dotted-note trill with anticipation normally stops on t dot and is played as follows:

Thus, the baroque trill, with the addition of the appoggiatura and the anticipation, is often only one-fourth of the note value indicated.

In the following instances, the mordent or trill is played as a triplet on the beat.

the third example, slower tempos allow the performance of grace notes as indicated, but faster tempos again demand a triplet on the beat, as above.

The baroque mordent, like the trill, usually begins with the upper note, unless already preceded by that note. Again, this upper note is not a grace note and must be played on the beat. In faster tempos, this often results in four even notes. In slower tempos, the mordent should retain its character.

Sonata in F Major

Sonata in D Minor

The *grupetto* or turn is usually interpreted in one of the following ways:

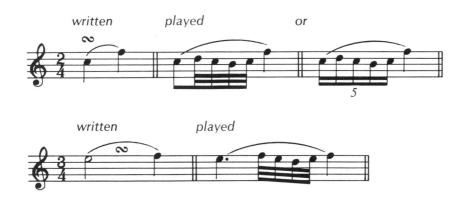

If the turn occurs in a dotted-note value, however, it is always played in the following rhythmic proportion:

Chromatic alterations in the turn are placed above or below the sign to indicate the desired change.

The baroque and the classic appoggiatura, written as small notes without the slash of a grace note, are usually accepted as having one-half the value of the note they are attached to. But editing often loses the composer's intent, so that the performer must decide when a grace note is truly intended. Also, these appoggiaturas are always slurred to the following tone, whether the slur is indicated or not.

Sonata in B Minor

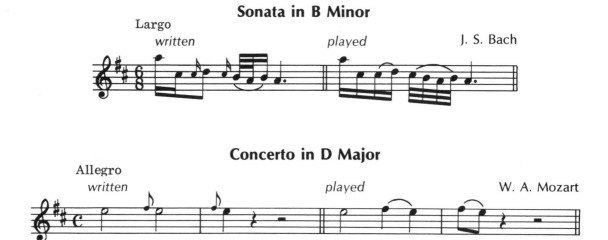

When attached to longer note values, especially in slower tempos, the appoggiatura is often more satisfactory as a note shorter than half the value of the following note.

Concerto in D Major

A two-to-one ratio is often recommended when the appoggiatura is attached to a dotted note, but usually a one-to-two ratio will prove more musically satisfactory.

Sonata in B Minor

Sonata in C Major

CHAPTER XI

PERFORMANCE ON OTHER FLUTES

THE E♭ FLUTE

The E♭ flute is often recommended for the child who is too small to handle the size of the concert flute, since all aspects of instruction regarding the C flute, including embouchure, fingering, and phrasing, apply equally to the E♭ instrument. The student must get used to hearing the transposition, however, in order correctly to judge embouchure placement, jaw, breath support, etc.; then he can adjust to the C flute later.

There are no method books for this instrument, unfortunately, so a regular flute method must be used, with teacher and student making the necessary aural adjustment. Group methods cannot ordinarily be used, but E♭ clarinet parts can be used in band rehearsals and performances, often with most satisfactory results. If a particular school program requires group instruction of unlike instruments, E♭ clarinet books may be used if the fingerings and some other aspects (including the range) are altered to suit the E♭ flute.

The possibilities of the E♭ flute for the professional flutist have barely been explored. Although the tone tends to be somewhat thinner than that of the concert flute yet not as brilliant or shrill as that of the piccolo in corresponding ranges, the E♭ flute would seem to be of great value in concert performance. Some extremely difficult orchestral passages in the highest octave, particularly in the softer dynamics,

*See pages 1 and 2 for written and transposed ranges.

could be facilitated by the use of the E♭ flute. Passages such as the Prokofiev example on page 62 become relatively easy when fingered a minor third lower, as do those involving scale and arpeggio passages to the highest D (D^4). Similarly, some of the low register passages written for piccolo might well be more satisfactorily performed on the E♭ flute.

In the search for new sounds and technical possibilities, the contemporary composer and the jazz musician alike would do well to familiarize themselves with the E♭ flute.

THE ALTO FLUTE IN G

The alto flute was a favorite instrument of Theobald Boehm. Because of its extended and beautifully mellow lower range, it is most used in its two lowest octaves. The top octave is rarely used, but all principles of performance on the concert flute apply also to the alto flute.

Again, the performer must practice the basic embouchure exercises to accustom himself to the transposition. The alto flute requires a greater quantity of air in performance than does the concert flute and is therefore not recommended for beginning students. This factor limits the length of phrases possible in performance, and also slightly affects the use of rapid or very acute articulation, since the alto flute tends to respond somewhat sluggishly, particularly in the lowest octave.

In this century the alto flute has been used more and more in symphonic literature. Two of the earliest examples are in Ravel's *Daphnis et Chloé* suite and Stravinsky's *Le Sacre du Printemps*. There is a limited amount of solo literature available for the alto flute, including excellent transcriptions of some of the concert flute repertoire. Use of the alto flute in ensemble literature, jazz, and popular music has recently increased, but there is a place for much more exploitation of this instrument. Its sensitive tone, unfortunately, can be a disadvantage in orchestral scoring in other than solo passages, but in small ensembles or when electronically amplified, it is superbly rich.

THE BASS FLUTE IN C

Sounding an octave lower than the concert flute, the bass flute extends the range of the flute family down another fifth. Except for the remarks regarding literature, all comments referring to the alto flute are also true of the bass instrument. Because the embouchure hole may not be acoustically proportioned to the size of the rest of the instrument and remain playable, the bass flute is often very difficult to play in its lowest octave. Amplification in the recording studio or in some other circumstances can be a practical solution to this problem. One of the most promising recent experiments with the bass flute has been a process of building up the far wall of the embouchure hole, making it significantly easier to play. More experimentation in this direction by manufacturers may soon make the bass flute as popular as the alto flute has become.

THE PICCOLO

The piccolo is the same as the concert flute in principle, but embouchure placement is relative to the difference in size of the hole, and the concept of breath support is like adding another octave to the C flute.

Intonation factors that apply to the C flute (see p. 76) are also true of the piccolo but greatly exaggerated. The performer, therefore, must be extremely careful and sensitive in adjusting to problems of pitch. The tendency of the human ear to hear octaves "stretched" in order to sound comfortably in tune must be of particular concern to the piccolo artist. Conductors as well as performers frequently want to hear the high octave sharper than it should be, and an occasional check of these octaves with a strobo-tuner or similar device is highly recommended. This may prove to be a considerable surprise to the performer.

Lack of the foot-joint extension on the piccolo makes the written D^1 the lowest note available and also prevents the production of notes above written C^4, with the exception of written $C\#^4$, usually attainable with the alternate fingerings: 2 /1, or 2 4/1.

The alternate fingering for written Ab^3 (234/ 23Eb) is used almost exclusively, since this tone is difficult to produce and tends to be somewhat sharp. The alternate fingerings for written E^3: 12 /12, or 12 /12^B, are also used more frequently on the piccolo than on the concert flute for greater ease of control and security. All other trill, tremolando, and alternate fingerings are the same as those for the concert flute (pp. 26-27, 50-60, 62-65) where within the written range of the piccolo.

It is only in the manufacture of piccolos that wood is used to any great extent. The wood piccolo is usually preferred to metal because of its superior tone quality, when made with a conical bore. The quality is significantly mellower and fuller, although intonation is slightly less stable and the top octave is somewhat harder to produce.

The metal cylindrical-bore piccolo is more popular with school organizations, and rightfully so, because of its more stable intonation and ease of tone production. These factors well offset the more shrill and thin tone of the metal instrument in comparison to the wooden model. The professional piccolo artist often employs both the conical-bore wood piccolo and the cylindrical-bore metal instrument, relying on each for its particular advantages.

As in the case of the metal C flute, the metal piccolo is available in several combinations of silver or plating (see pp. 2-3). Various combinations of these materials are also available in piccolos, such as wooden body and metal head-joint, wooden head-joint and metal body, metal head-joint with wood, ivory, or plastic embouchure plate. In addition, the recent use of Ebonite and other plastic materials in piccolo construction has proved surprisingly successful.

When purchasing a student instrument, the buyer should check the design and adjustment of the G# key and the trill keys very carefully. The minute size of the instrument can be a serious problem in design and manufacturing. For example, if the G# key opens too much or is of faulty design, it will shift the entire rod system when depressed. Likewise, trill keys on some piccolos have been designed in such a manner that the fingers of an average-sized right hand cannot depress the keys of that hand without slightly opening the trill keys or shifting the key rods. In either case, satisfactory performance is impossible to attain.

It should also be mentioned that the Db piccolo, although standard for band use some years ago, is rapidly becoming obsolete. Almost all band parts are now published for C piccolo. In the rare instance when a C part is not available, the transposition is relatively simple, even for the average student performer.

Doubling on piccolo and flute, in spite of their considerable similarities, can be a problem for student and professional alike. The professional piccolo artist, who usually serves also as third flutist, must constantly guard against concentrating on his piccolo skill to the detriment of his flute-playing ability. The difference in embouchure, although slight, will affect his tone quality and facility on the flute unless equal time is devoted to both instruments, with a concentrated effort directed to analyzing and controlling the minor adjustments of embouchure, jaw, breath support, and throat necessary for optimum performance. For the student, these problems are compounded by the tendency to concentrate solely on the piccolo during football season. The common difficulties of the average flute student, such as tight embouchure, small aperture in the lips, and closed throat, are all encouraged when the student confines himself to playing the piccolo at the expense of his development as a flutist. The solution, again, is at least equal time spent in flute study. Two additional problems face the student who concentrates too much on the piccolo. One is the octave transposition, which causes aural uncertainty when returning to the flute; the other is the faster and easier response of the piccolo in all types of articulation, hindering facility and clarity of articulation on the concert flute. All students, however, should be familiar with the piccolo, and in those instances where the student's problem is an infirm embouchure on the flute, the piccolo may prove to be a great aid in his development.

Although the piccolo is used a great deal in orchestra, band, and ensemble literature, solo literature is both scarce and disappointing. There are some excellent concerti of Vivaldi, as well as a few contemporary works. The balance is primarily of a novelty nature: polkas, scherzos, themes and variations in the most trite nineteenth-century style.

Since the question of starting beginners on the piccolo does occasionally arise, the answer is that, for the beginner, the importance of the piccolo in relation to the concert flute is in direct proportion to the space devoted to each in this text.

BIBLIOGRAPHY

ACOUSTICS

Bartholemew, Wilmer T., *Acoustics of Music* (New York: Prentice Hall, 1946).

Culver, Charles, *Musical Acoustics* (New York: McGraw-Hill, 1956).

Jeans, Sir James, *Science and Music* (New York: Oxford University Press, 1951).

HISTORY AND DEVELOPMENT

Baasch, Robert J., "The Flute: Yesterday and To-day," *Woodwind* (Nov., 1954, p. 6; Dec., 1954, p. 6; Jan., 1955, p. 6).

Boehm, Theobald, *The Flute and Flute Playing* (New York: Dover, 1964).

de Lorenzo, Lenardo, *My Complete Story of the Flute* (New York: Citadel Press, 1951).

Fitzgibbon, H. Macaulay, *The Story of the Flute* (New York: Charles Scribner's Sons, 1914).

Girard, Adrien, *Histoire et Richesses de la Flûte* (Paris: Librairie Gründ, 1953).

Quantz, Johann J., *Versuch einer Anweisung, die flûte traversière zu spielen* (Berlin:1789) facsimile, (Berlin: Bärenreiter, 1953).

Rockstro, Richard S., *The Flute* (London: Rudall, Carte & Co., 1890; rev., 1920).

Welch, Christopher, *History of the Boehm Flute* (New York: facsimile ed.).

PERFORMANCE AND PEDAGOGY

Cavally, Robert, *Comprehensive Trill Fingerings For Flute* (Elkhart, Ind.: W. T. Armstrong Co., 1960).

Chapman, F. B., *Flute Technique* (New York: Oxford University Press, 1951).

Eisonson, Jon, "Diaphragmatic Breathing," *Symphony* (March, 1951, p. 8).

Globus, Rudo S., (Ed.), *The Woodwind Anthology* (New York: Woodwind Magazine, 1952).

Gray, Gary, *Tone Production and Resonance* (Elkhart, Ind.: W. T. Armstrong Co.).

Hall, J. and E. Kent, *The Effect of Temperature on the Tuning Standards of Wind Instruments* (Elkhart, Ind.,: C. G. Conn, Ltd.).

Hauenstein, Nelson, *The Flute, Tonguing and Articulation* (Elkhart, Ind.: W. T. Armstrong Co.).

Hosmer, James B., "The Vibrato Question," *Woodwind* (Oct., 1949, p. 5).

Hotteterre, Jacques, *Principes de la Flûte Traversière* (Paris: 1728), (facsimile, Kassel, 1941).

Kujala, Walfrid, *The Flute, Position and Balance* (Elkhart, Ind.: W. T. Armstrong Co.).

Laurent, Georges, "On Playing the Flute," *Symphony* (March, 1950, p. 10).

————. "Playing Legato on the Flute," *Symphony* (Feb., 1952, p. 11).

Marx, Josef, "The Truth About Vibrato, a Musicologist Views its Development," *Woodwind* (4:4, Nov., 1951).

Maxym, Stephen, "The Technique of Breathing for Wind Instruments," *Woodwind* (Jan.-April, 1953).

Moyse, Marcel, "On Flute Playing," *Symphony* (June, (1949, p. 5; July, 1949, p. 7).

————. "The Unsolvable Problem, Considerations on Flute Vibrato," *Woodwind* (March, 1950; April, 1950; May, 1950).

North, Charles K., *Charts of Fingering of the Boehm Flute* (Boston: Cundy-Bettoney).

Opperman, George, "The Vibrato Problem, The Seashore Study Applied," *Woodwind* (Feb., 1950; March, 1950).

Pellerite, James J., *A Modern Guide to Fingerings for the Flute* (Bloomington, Ind.: Zālo Publications, 1964).

Sprenkle, Robert, "Wind Instrument Vibrato,"*Symphony* (Feb., 1951, p. 9).

Stevens, Roger S., *Artistic Flute Technique and Study* (Hollywood: Highland Music Co., 1967).

Vornholt, David, *Vibrato* (Elkhart, Ind.: W. T. Armstrong Co.).

Wilkins, Frederick, "Flute Vibrato," *Connchord* (Oct., 1961).

———— . *The Flutists Guide* (Elkhart, Ind.: 1957).

———— . "Speed of Flute Vibrato," *Connchord* (Jan., 1962).

REPAIR AND MAINTENANCE

Brand, Erick D., *Band Instrument Repairing Manual* (Elkhart, Ind.: Erick D. Brand, 1946).

Conn, Co., C. G., *Practical Problems in Building Wind Instruments* (Elkhart, Ind.: C. G. Conn Co., 1942).

Kirschner, Frederick, *Encyclopedia of Band Instrument Repairing* (New York: Music Trade Review, 1962).

Tiede, Clayton H. T., *Practical Band Instrument Repair Manual* (Dubuque, Iowa: Wm. C. Brown, 1962).

SELECTED MUSIC LITERATURE
GRADE I

Methods

Altes, Henri, *Complete Method* (Paris: Leduc).

Eck, Emil, *Eck Method* (Belwin).

Kincaid, William, *The Art and Practice of Modern Flute Technique* (New York, MCA Music, 1968).

Taffanel-Gaubert, *Complete Flute Method* (Leduc).

Wagner, Ernest, *Flute Method* (Carl Fischer).

Solos

Everybody's Favorite Flute Solos, No. 83 (Amsco).

Moyse, L., *40 Pieces in Progressive Order for Beginning Flutists* (G. Schirmer).

GRADE II

Studies

Cavally, Robert, *Melodious and Progressive Studies for Flute, Book I* (Southern Music).

Eck, Emil, *Tone Development* (Belwin).

Solos

Bach-Barrère, *Arioso* (G. Schirmer).

Moyse, L., *Album of Sonatinas for Flute* (G Schirmer).

Mozart-Isaac, *Andante from Piano Sonata No. 1* (Carl Fischer).

Duets

Favorite Flute Duets (Cundy-Bettoney).

Koehler, *40 Progressive Duets, Vol. 1* (Carl Fischer).

Voxman, H., *Selected Flute Duets, Vol. 1* (Rubank).

GRADE III

Studies

Andersen, J., *24 Studies, Op. 33* (Carl Fischer).

Berbiguier, *Eighteen Exercises* (Carl Fischer).

Moyse, M., *Daily Exercises* (Leduc).

———— . *Scales and Arpeggios* (Leduc).

Platonov, *30 Studies* (International).

Solos

Handel, G. F., *Sonatas* (Southern Music).

Hotteterre, J., *Suite in D Major* (Ricordi).

Latham, W. P., *Suite in Baroque Style* (Summy-Birchard).

Loeillet, J. B., *Sonata No. 7* (Lemoine).

Mozart-Boehm, *Andante, Op. 86* (Cundy-Bettoney).

Mozart, W. A., *Two Sonatinas* (Peters).

Voxman, H., ed., *Concert and Contest Collection for Flute* (Rubank).

Duets

Koehler, *40 Progressive Duets, Vol. II* (Carl Fischer).

Soussman, *Twelve Duets, Op. 53* (International).

Voxman, H., ed., *Selected Flute Duets, Vol. II* (Rubank).

GRADE IV

Studies

Boehm, Th., *12 Studies, Op. 15* (Carl Fischer).

Furstenau, A. B., *Studies, Op. 125* (Belwin).

Prill, Emil, *24 Studies, Op. 12* (Carl Fischer).

Soussman-Popp, *24 Grand Studies* (Part III of Complete Method) (Carl Fischer).

Solos

Bate, Stanley, *Sonatina* (Schott).

Bloch, E., *Suite Modale* (Broude Bros.).

Debussy, C., *Syrinx* (Elkan-Vogel).

Grétry, A. E. M., *Concerto in C* (Southern Music).

Handel, G. F., *Concerto in D* (Möseler).

Kennan, Kent, *Night Soliloquy* (Carl Fischer).

Koechlin, Ch., *Fourteen Pieces for Flute and Piano* (Salabert).

Platti, G. *Sonata No. 3 in A* (Schott).

Purcell, H., *Dance Suite* (E. C. Schirmer).

Scarlatti, A., *Suite* (Boosey-Hawkes).

Selected Flute Solos, No. 101 (Amsco).

Telemann, G. P., *Concerto in D* (Leuckart).

———— . *Suite in A Minor* (Southern Music).

Tershak, A., *Murillo; Allegro de Concert, Op. 138* (Byron-Douglas).

Vivaldi, A., *Concerto in F* (Peters).

Duets

Briccialdi, L., *Dialogues, Op. 132* (Belwin).
Mattheson, J., *Four Sonatas, Op. 1* (Nagel).
Telemann, G. P., *Six Canonic Sonatas* (International).

GRADE V

Studies

Boehm-Wummer, *24 Etudes, Op. 26* (Carl Fischer).
Moyse, M., *Mechanism; Chromaticism* (Leduc).
———. *20 Studies Based on Kreutzer* (Leduc).
Prill, Emil., *Orchestra Studies* (Jack Spratt).
Torchio, *Orchestra Studies* (2 vols.) (Ricordi).

Solos

Bach, C. P. E., *Concerto in A* (International).
———. *Sonata in A Minor* (Carl Fischer).
Blavet, M., *Sonatas* (Cundy-Bettoney).
Boccherini, L., *Concerto in D* (Southern Music).
Eitler, M., *Sentimiento Indefinido* (Mercury).
Frederick The Great, *Sonatas* (2 vols.) (Breitkopf and Härtel).
Gaubert, Ph., *Fantasie* (Salabert).
Gluck, C., *Concerto in G* (Peters).
Hue, Georges, *Fantasie* (Salabert).
Mozart, W. A., *Concertos in G and D* (G. Schirmer).
Pergolesi, L., *Concerto in G* (International).
———. *Concerto in D* (International).
Telemann, G. P., *Sonatas* (G. Schirmer).

Duets

Kuhlau, F., *Duets,* Op. 10, 80, 81, 102, etc., (International).

GRADE VI

Studies

Andersen, J., *24 Studies, Op. 15* (Carl Fischer).
———. *24 Technical Etudes, Op. 63* (Southern Music).
Moyse, M., *Technical Studies and Exercises* (Leduc).
———. *Ten Studies Based on Kessler* (Leduc).
Platonov, *24 Studies* (International).

Solos

Bach, J. S., *Sonatas* (Boston Music).
———. *Suite in B Minor* (Cundy-Bettoney).
Enesco, G., *Cantabile et Presto* (Boosey and Hawkes).
Fauré, G., *Fantasie, Op. 79* (Belwin).
Griffes, Ch., *Poem* (G. Schirmer).
Haydn, J., *Concerto in D* (Southern Music).
Hindemith, P., *Sonata* (Associated).
Ibert, J., *Pièce pour Flute Seule* (Leduc).
Milhaud, D., *Sonatine* (Elkan-Vogel).
Molique, G., *Concerto in D Minor* (Southern Music).
Quantz, J., *Concerto in G* (Southern Music).
Roussel, J. J., *Jouers de Flûte* (Durand).
Stevens, H., *Sonatina* (Broude Bros.).
Stringfield, L., *Mountain Dawn* (Edition Musicus).

GRADE VII

Studies

Jean-Jean, Paul, *Etudes Modernes* (Leduc).
Moyse, M., *12 Studies After Chopin* (Leduc).
———. *25 Studies of Virtuosity After Czerny* (Leduc).
Shostakovich, D., *Orchestral Studies* (Leeds).
Strauss, R., *Orchestral Studies* (Cundy-Bettoney).
Wagner, R., *Orchestral Studies* (International).

Solos

Boughton, R., *Concerto in D* (Boosey-Hawkes).
Dahl, Ingolf, *Variations on a Swedish Folk Tune* (New Music).
Dutilleux, H., *Sonatine* (Leduc).
Goosens, E., *Three Pictures* (Chester).
Ibert, J., *Jeux* (Leduc).
Kerr, H., *Suite* (Associated).
Martin, F., *Ballade* (Universal).
Martinu, B., *Sonata* (Associated).
Piston, W., *Sonata* (Associated).
Poulenc, F., *Sonata* (Chester).
Quantz, J., *Concerto in D* (Peters).
Schulhoff, E., *Sonata* (Chester).
Tomasi, H., *Concertino in E* (Costallat).

Duets

Hindemith, P., *Canonic Sonata, Op. 31, No. 3* (Schott).
Koechlin, Ch., *Sonata, Op. 75* (Senart).
Mozart, W. A., *Six Duets* (Cundy-Bettoney).

GRADE VIII

Studies

Andersen, J., *24 Virtuosity Studies, Op. 60* (Southern Music).
Karg-Elert, *30 Caprices, Op. 107* (Cundy-Bettoney). (Also contained in *The Modern Flutist,* publ. by Southern Music).
Moyse, M. *Ten Studies After Wieniawsky* (Leduc).
———. *20 Exercises and Studies; Great Slurs, Trills, etc.* (Leduc).
Moyse, M., *28 Studies of Virtuosity* (Leduc).

Solos

Alwyn, W., *Divertimento* (Boosey-Hawkes).
Bozza, E., *Agrestide* (Leduc).
Casella, A., *Sicilienne et Burlesque* (Evette & Schaffer).
Ibert, J., *Concerto* (Leduc).
Koechlin, Ch., *Sonata, Op. 52* (Senart).
Passani, *Concerto* (Costallat).
Pendleton, E., *Concerto Alpestre* (Ars Musica).
Prokofiev, S., *Sonata, Op. 94* (International).
Schubert, F., *Introduction and Variations on "Ihr Blümlein alle", Op. 160* (Breitkopf and Härtel).
Tomasi, H., *Concerto in F* (Leduc).